Praise for *Journalese*

"Good editors keep trying to kill clichés, but clichés outlive editors. So Paul Dickson and Robert Skole have given clichés a good look—up close and personal, as a cliché clod might say. *Journalese* isn't a laff-a-minute book: it's a smile-every-30-seconds book. I'm Mervin Block, and I approve this book—heartily."
　　—**Mervin Block**, author of *Weighing Anchors*

"Never has the deciphering of newspeak into plain English been so hilarious. *Journalese* shows how the power of original phrasing fuels great reporting. To mimic Dickson and Skole, the 'deep translation' of 'a must-read for reporters' is 'Listen up, journalists, your trite, impersonal, clichés have got to go.'"
　　—**Suzette Martinez Standring**, award-winning author of *The Art of Column Writing*

"*Journalese* is a handy guide to the good, the bad, the beautiful, and the ugly of that special language that most of us read and hear every day. The authors' insights will change the way you interpret the news."
　　—**Richard Lederer**, author of *Lederer on Language*

"I always knew Ambrose Bierce was the pseudonym of Paul Dickson and Robert Skole ... and I enjoyed *Journalese* just as much as *The Devil's Dictionary*."
　　—**Lewis Burke Frumkes**, author of *Favorite Words of Famous People* and *Metapunctuation*

"Anyone wrestling with English as a second language will find this book a key to understanding a third English language, journalese. It's a delightful dictionary for foreign correspondents, students, business people and all others who follow international news."
　　—**Erik Mellgren**, senior staff writer, *Ny Teknik*, Stockholm

Journalese

{ A Dictionary for Deciphering the News }

PAUL DICKSON AND ROBERT SKOLE

Marion Street Press

Portland, Oregon

This book is dedicated to those sharp-eyed editors who blue-penciled, re-wrote, revised, tossed back, and in other ways rescued us from much, but not all, of the most outrageous journalese in our writings over the years. And to the keenest of all, Nancy and Monika.

Published by Marion Street Press
4207 S.E. Woodstock Blvd. # 168
Portland, OR 97206-6267
USA
http://www.marionstreetpress.com/

Orders and review copies: (800) 888-4741

Printed in the United States of America
ISBN 978-1-936863-12-9

Library of Congress Cataloging-in-Publication Data pending

Introduction

"Word on Journalism Street is that somebody out there is writing a dictionary of journalese," is what deputy editor Frank Fellone wrote in the *Arkansas Democrat-Gazette* on March 1, 2011.

"This," he said, "is cause for either celebration or dread.

"Celebration because if this dictionary is ever published, every news writer will have at hand a book of what not to do. Dread because a dictionary of journalese might have the effect of legitimizing this gruesome body of language particular to this craft, and by legitimizing it spread its use."

He added in plain English, devoid of journalese: "Yuck to that."

Fallone we presume was alluding to the slim volume that you now hold in your hands and he heard about it because of an invitation on the MizzouMafia Listserv, for graduates of the University of Missouri School of Journalism and for any others in the trade. The invitation was for journalists' examples of journalese, and was sent by Robert Skole, a proud graduate of the Mizzou J-School.

Now that the book has been published —the very first book to be titled *Journalese*—there is neither cause for celebration nor dread, because it was never our intention to stamp out journalese nor to bless it. Our role was to describe and define it and, in the process, perhaps spike—or at least skewer—some of its more overwrought examples. As a dictionary it is descriptive rather than proscriptive.

So what is this thing called journalese but also named newspaperese, newspeak and mediaspeak?

Journalese is the particular code in which journalists report a story. It is a pattern of language—a jargon—that never appears in normal conversation. Or as Fallone put it: "Language you'd never use at a party when trying to impress a pretty girl." Nevertheless it fills our newspapers, magazines, websites and blogs, is broadcast over the air, snaked into our homes through a cable and beamed down by satellite. Increasingly (that's an adverbial opener, a classic journalese way to start a sentence), it is coming in on devices with names unknown a half-decade ago—smart phone, Kindle, Nook, iPad, you name it. But even as the delivery systems change the code remains in place.

The more the world changes the more journalese stays the same. Temperatures still soar. Costs still skyrocket. Tornadoes still cut swaths, leaving rescue workers to sift through the rubble and survivors searching for answers. Heated debates are still carried out before packed auditoriums. Campaign funds are still war chests, the cost of a project is still its price tag, and before said project can start it needs a green light. As a former UPI bureau chief Bill Mead observed, "Grieving families still wait, in the rain, for word about loved ones trapped underground by the coal mine disaster. As in decades past, grizzled veterans lead teams to victory, as do fresh-faced rookies."

Of course, sports writing could not exist without its own bottomless reservoir of journalese. Reporters covering the first Olympic Games undoubtedly had competitors chucking the javelin, sailing over the hurdles, and superbly spinning the discus. And it has flourished ever since. Sports have been presented and defined since newspaper dispatches were transmitted by telegraph wire in the 19th Century. Then came radio broadcasters who had to create their own—often colorful—ways of bringing games to life. We will not cover sports journalese *per se* in this book; because the language of sports and sports journalese are so often one in the same. Gene Collier, of the *Pittsburgh Post-Gazette*, awards the annual "Trite Trophy: A cliché for all (sporting) seasons." This is a valuable contribution to the understanding of journalese.

Journalese has been described with just about every imaginable negative adjective: from awful to zippy. It has been denounced from the earliest mentions of the term "journalese". A British columnist, "The Lounger," in the Nov. 15, 1890 issue of *The Critic: A Weekly Review of Literature and the Arts*, harrumphed: "In literature as in travel Sir Richard Burton's work was the most single-handed. He wrote the worst style in the world—the vilest in an age of villainies: a compost of archaisms and neologisms, of slang and English that has faded out of life—an English that is only English to the adept in journalese."

Journalese has even been described poetically, according to British author Bevis Hillier. In a book review in the *Spectator*, Aug, 26, 2006, he wrote: "When people use the word 'journalese', they always do so pejoratively. They are not thinking of James Cameron, Bernard Levin or Walter Winchell. They mean a style that traffics in clichés. The poet B. I. Isherville has derided that kind of writing: 'Where every heresy is rank, And every rank is serried; Where every crook is hatchet-faced, And every hatchet buried.'"

But there is also some praise of Journalese: even being described as artistic, exquisite and Corinthian (see "Adjectives Describe Journalese, A to Z").

An Internet search in early 2012 offered only one hit for "honest journalese." However, there were none for "dishonest journalese" in quotes, and 10 hits without quotes, in citations of when journalese might be dishonest. This may help reporters and editors maintain a humble sense of professional neutrality and objectivity, if they ever thought about it when making use of journalese.

The critics of journalese are legion—most notably among those who write about writing and care about style. "In general, journalese is the tone of contrived excitement," wrote Wilson Follett, in his *Modern American Usage,* more than a half a century ago: "When the facts by themselves do not make the reader's pulse beat faster, the journalist thinks it is his duty to apply the spur and whip of breathless phrases." In *On Writing Well*, which was first published in 1976, William Zinnser called journalese "the death of freshness in anybody's style." He explained in the 2006 revision of that classic work: "It's the common currency of newspapers and of magazines like *People*— a mixture of cheap words, made-up words and clichés that have become so pervasive that a writer can hardly help using them. You must fight these phrases or you'll sound like every hack. You'll never make your mark as a writer unless you develop a respect for words and a curiosity about their shades of meaning that is almost obsessive. The English language is rich in strong and supple words. Take the time to root around and find the ones you want."

Journalese is not new. The Old and New Testaments wax so rich with journalese—abide, begat, smite and, verily, hundreds more— that it has been called "Gospel journalese".

One of the earliest dictionary definitions was in the 1872 edition of *Merriam-Webster*, which defined it simply: "a style of writing held to be characteristic of newspapers." Rudyard Kipling described a

Kansas City paper's story of a rescue as "joyous journalese", in *Captains Courageous*, published in 1897. This illustrates that the word "journalese" was then well-understood by the broad public.

But journalese itself has rarely been "joyously" accepted, even though widely used. It has been identified as a weakness of journalism for more than a century. An early diatribe from the San Francisco *Evening Bulletin*, May 13, 1882, quoting the *Saturday Review of Literature*:

> Newspaper Language: Nothing can be less poetical, or more stereotyped, than the construction of newspaper English. Men who write in a hurry on hackneyed subjects, and who have nothing new to say, naturally use the well-worn molds of newspaper prose. Certain sentences, certain expressions, like 'conspicuous by its absence' are remorselessly employed, and the regular pressman is even angry if any of his contemporaries choose to abandon these old favorites of the public, and to write as if journalism were a branch of literature. Just as the industrious and ingenious workingman is 'rattened' and 'picketed' by working men who think the standard of skill quite high enough already, so the journalist who does not wish, if he can avoid it, to write 'journalese' is detested by hardened old hands."

So it was and so it is today. Reporter Mike Berry sized it up in an *Orlando Sentinel* opinion piece aptly titled, "Life Is A Cliché, A No-Win Situation, An Uphill Battle That Sounds The Alarm For A Wake-Up Call (If You Know What We Mean.)." "It's a kind of shorthand the job inflicts upon us, from covering too many of the same types of stories. We strive to be creative, but a cliché is like an old sweatshirt always there in the closet of our vocabulary, well-worn, easy to slip on, comfortable."

Mike Feinsilber, the writing coach in the Washington Bureau of The Associated Press, said of these words used only by news writers: "They're handy but they're flat, lifeless, uninspired, imprecise." Feinsilber has also identified a subspecies of journalese: "phrases that brought an inner smile when first encountered—but that was a thousand encounters ago. You remember 'on steroids,' as in, 'The deficit used to be big but this is a deficit on steroids'?"

The darker side of journalese is that it can create stereotypes and act as a shortcut away from accuracy. As Dharma Adhikari, a journalist from Nepal, a graduate of the University of Missouri School of Journalism and currently teaching at Georgia Southern University, wrote in a piece entitled, "(Un)reading journalese" in the Nepal newspaper *Republica,* Aug. 29, 2010: "If the world's best newspapers use journalese, it must be good for us! Almost every story about this country in the foreign newswires or *The New York Times* reminds us that Nepal is 'a tiny Himalayan country flanked by China and India.' Our newspapers get it and do not hesitate to repeat it. Wait a minute: what makes us tiny? The truth is, more than half the world's 200 nations are smaller than Nepal. The international journalese has charmed us into unwittingly accepting that we are 'remote', 'poverty-infested', and a 'failed-state', or living on 'less than half a dollar a day'."

Also, on the negative side there is an opinion being voiced that journalese is one of the factors in the loss of newspaper readership. John E. McIntyre, the former assistant managing editor for *The Baltimore Sun* copy desk and now a language blogger on that newspaper's website, wrote in his February 8, 2012 blog that he was about to repeat something he had been trying to get journalists to hear for twenty years. "One reason that newspaper journalism has been faltering is the stubborn adherence of journalists to a language no one else uses. The readers who are comfortable with journalese, who formed the newspaper habit early, are climbing the golden staircase, and the succeeding generations are not developing the habit. Why? One reason might well be that journalese sounds odd and unappealing to them."

The authors of this book, both men with journalistic backgrounds (Skole was once Dickson's boss in a Washington news bureau) do not suggest that we are innocents who have never committed high journalese. Quite the contrary, anyone willing to look through the several million words the two of us have had published in our collective 150+ years on earth will find examples galore—some, perhaps, even more outlandish than anything found in this book.

With this know-how, we have also been culling the printed and electronic world for some 25 years and, like stamp collectors, we needed a time and a place to show off our collection.

That said, not all journalese and media euphemism is bad or to be avoided at all costs—or, as the journalistic cliché goes "avoided like the plague." There are those who have defended journalese although they are not easy to find. The argument is simple and straightforward and was stated way back in 1953 in an Associated Press piece entitled, "Journalese Approved by English Professors" in which two professors gave journalese their "stamp of approval." One was Dr. E. Glenn Griffin of Purdue University who said, "Newspaper English is all right. Journalese is all right because it is serving its purpose."

Case in point. Obituary notices used to carry such phrases as "died of natural causes after a long illness" which is a euphemistic way of not mentioning cancer or, increasingly, Alzheimer's, and "died unexpectedly after a short illness," meaning a stroke or heart attack. These were simply kindnesses and courtesies to families who would prefer not to see the name of a disease in print. Today, it is common to give the precise cause of death. But journalese euphemisms are still alive in obituaries, and were raised to an art form in the British press by the late Hugh Massingberd, of *The Daily Telegraph*, who gave us such classics as "convivial", meaning habitually drunk, or "a powerful negotiator" for a bully.

Finally, there is a distinction to be made between pure cliché and a higher level of euphemism. In 1972 Russell Baker of *The New York Times* wrote an essay on the "idiom of praise" which reporters used when covering politicians. Baker said that when a reporter called a politician a "pragmatist" he was describing an unprincipled opportunist who will do whatever it takes to get re-elected. "To the reporters," Baker wrote, "public men differ from common humanity, for their ranks do not include anyone of mean spirit or cold heart. Mean-spirited, cold-hearted men are almost always, in political journaling as 'tough-minded,' 'levelheaded' and 'realistic'."

To highlight that a journalese entry in this book can be a euphemism for something other than its accepted definition, that it may mean something devious or a reporter's own code, we will label such words with the notation **DEEP TRANSLATION**.

We also define some words that we identify as "**JOURNOSPEAK**," the inside lingo that journalists use among themselves, such as "lede," for the leading sentences or the first "graf" of a story, or "30," meaning the end of a text or message. This is not what is generally described as journalese. A reporter or editor slipping such words into a story will delight old-timers.

We gather into sidebars (and that's **JOURNOSPEAK**, in this case, for special sections) words that are used covering specific fields or events, such as "Plat du Journalese," the language of restaurant and food critics, or "Election Journalese," which is unavoidable, whether it's an election for town council or the U.S. president, or "Headlinese," short, punchy, handy words that everyone understands, but which are rarely used outside of headlines.

Illustrating our point that journalese is invaluable to journalists, sharp-eyed readers will certainly spot our own use of journalese in this book. One might say it's egg on our faces, as we say in journalese.

Columnist John Leo proudly says he is "a recognized expert on journalese." His book, *Two Steps Ahead of the Thought Police*, published in 1998, contains an essay titled "Journalese, an Englishlike language." Describing this art as "the arcane lingo of reporters and pundits," he closes with: "Journalese is an omnipresent, well-respected, oft-hyphenated and need-driven language that slashes through the dull patina of mundane objectivity and lets readers know what you really think. Where would we be without it?"

We fully agree.

And now, welcome to the joys of journalese.

A number of. Two to infinity. A 1989 letter to *The Washington Post* from reader William J. Karppi listed a few of his favorite examples of journalese: "And finally, my favorite: 'a number of' as in a number of people gathered in front of the embassy. That's an indisputable count, isn't it?"

A sense of. Obligatory question when a television reporter doesn't have a solid question, as "Can you give me a sense of what's behind the Mayor's appointment of his cousin as chief of parking ticket fines?"

A while back. "Journalese for more months than I want to say," according to "The Word" columnist Jan Freeman, in *The Boston Globe*, Mar. 5, 2000.

According to scattered reports. Tom Allen, who reported for the *Bridgeport Herald*, recalled that when he first read this in his paper he envisioned reporters running around to town offices and neighborhoods, picking up reports scattered everywhere.

Across the pond. The UK in the U.S.; the U.S. in the UK. Magazine writer Randy Rieland commented on the eve of the April 29, 2011, Royal Wedding: "We could put a serious dent in the national debt if everyone kicked in a buck every time someone on TV utters the phrase 'across the pond' this week."

Activist. Not a bureaucrat. Anyone who voices an opinion in public. Or as contributor Charlie Eckhardt offers: "Someone with a machine gun or a bomb who espouses a cause with which the newsman agrees." If no agreement, the person is a "terrorist."

Active. Can be used to explain the literal meaning, or, **DEEP**

TRANSLATION: Overdoes it. To be "active socially" is to drink heavily.

Active crime scene. Cops are there.

Activity. TV weather word that means nothing but sounds important. "We can expect some thunderstorm activity in the next 72 hours." Newspapers still refer to them as plain old thunderstorms.

Actually. Reporter wants to assure you this is the real stuff, unlike the rest of the story. Renée Loth, former editorial page editor of *The Boston Globe,* in a column Jan. 1, 2011, headlined "11 things we can live without in '11", included: "Actually. This filler adverb—the new 'really'—is suddenly being misused everywhere. 'She's not actually in right now.' 'We're actually closed Sunday.' Arrgh! The word grates on the inner ear like aural sandpaper." It obviously doesn't grate on *Globe* copy-editors' eyes or ears, since "actually" was used in eight *Globe* stories that day. TV news reporters are obliged to tell viewers they are "actually" doing something. Diane Sawyer, seen standing knee-deep in water, pointed out to viewers, in case they could not believe their eyes, that she was "actually" standing in the flooding Mississippi.

Adamant. Depending on whether the reporter or editor likes the guy, it means either pig-headed or sticking firmly to principles. "Adamant abortion foes look for a candidate," headlined a *Chicago Tribune* story, July 2, 1995.

ADJECTIVES DESCRIBE JOURNALESE, FROM A TO Z

Here is a very short list of adjectives describing journalese found in books, newspapers, magazines, on the Web—going back some 130 years.

artistic	interesting
awful	lively
bad	lurid
cheap	meretricious
choppy	mock-heroic
coarse	outmoded
colourful	pedestrian
Corinthian	print
cynical	ranker
delightful	scientific
dreary	shirt-sleeve
exuberant	slipshod
exquisite	spiced
first-rate	spiritless
flippant	stilted
florid	straight
frank	tabloid
Gospel	uncouth
graceless	unfair
hack	vivid
horrible	vulgar
imprecise	zippy

Adult. Dirty, as applied to bookstores, magazines and movies.

Adult beverage. Booze.

Adventurous. In travel stories, someone who went someplace few people go to. **DEEP TRANSLATION:** One who has slept with everyone.

Adversity. When used in sports, it's when an athlete has a past including theft and probation.

Advocate. Unlike activists, who often show up on the side of the environment and animal rights, advocates are more committed to civil rights, the consumer or the homeless. But a "homeless advocate," one reader told *Time* magazine, "always reminds me of an attorney sleeping in a dumpster."

Advocacy group. An organization promoting something, often with a name that is benign or totally misleading. If its position is not clearly identified, the reporter approves of it. Otherwise, it gets labeled, such as "far-right, ultra-conservative Genghis Khan supporters..." or "Leninist-inspired, far-left radicals...." *The Dallas Morning News* on Jan. 26, 2011, reported that the "consumer advocacy group Texas Watch" released a report saying, "The Texas Supreme Court over the last decade has morphed into an activist court driven by ideology and acting to benefit corporate interests."

Aesthetic. Arts reporters' spelling of "art". The *Los Angeles Times*, describing a designer's new swimsuit line, May 22, 2011, wrote: "Their brand, which launched its first collection in 2010, combines a carefree athletic and colorful aesthetic with seamless, hardware-free suits whose prints and colors are inspired mostly by the sisters' travels abroad." Now you know what aesthetics are.

After. "Kimberley Davies suffered the injury after jumping about 15 feet from a helicopter." What can that "after" possibly mean? First she jumped 15 feet and then somebody came along and kicked her? No, she suffered the injury when she jumped from the helicopter. Hence:

Aftermath. Just about anything following anything, whether connected or not. Jan Freeman, in "The Word" column in *The Boston Globe*, Nov. 7, 2004, explained: "Much of the world is involved in the long aftermath of the Iraq invasion, Red Sox fans are still in the aftermath of last month's World Series victory, and there are tiny little aftermaths all around. In journalese, especially, many an aftermath is just a fleeting connection between one moment and another." Jan Freeman did not add that school kids know that aftermath comes lunch, recess or another class.

Age-related. Accidents or incidents involving either teen-agers or geezers.

Aging. Anyone older than the reporter's father and not confounding time by growing younger, such as an aging bus fleet, aging boomers, aging school buildings. "An aging cargo handler was sentenced to life in prison..." reported AP, Feb.18, 2011, about a plot to blow up JFK airport. The man was 67. Even if he were 21, he'd be aging, since on his next birthday he'd be 22.

Aides. Assistants to politicians the reporter likes. Otherwise, they are hacks or coat-holders.

Ailing. When applied to a world leader or important politician, ailing means dying; but when applied to a professional athlete it usually refers to a torn rotator cuff or pulled Achilles tendon (two ailments which it would appear only come to those in professional sports). It is also what pundits say about newspapers and what was said about the American auto industry, which had been ailing for years before it rallied.

Alcohol. Term used when the ill-effects of its consumption are discussed. In festive stories, other words like cocktail, beer or wine are used.

Alert. Warning. Journalist Guy Keleny pointed out in the *London Independent* Jan. 17, 2004, "For while in normal English *alert* is most usually an adjective or adverb or verb—'Stay alert. If he calls you must alert me.'—in Journalese it is invariably a noun. 'Hoax call sparks terror alert.'"

Allegations. The stuff that's alleged, usually shocking.

Ambitious. Ponderous. A television reviewer's warning about any important eight-part series on public TV.

Alleged. Word used by reporters to prevent lawsuits. "The alleged murder took place when the victim was shot twice in the back."

Apocalyptic. Heading for disaster. The end of the world, but not really.

Appears. The reporter thinks so but isn't sure. Often used with "seems." "Gbagbo's rule appears to be nearing end as fighting rages." *The Denver Post* headlined this AP story (Apr. 2, 2011) with the lede, "Laurent Gbagbo's 10-year grip on the Ivory Coast seemed to be in its final hours Friday after fighters encircled both his residence and the presidential palace...." In this case, the reporter's prediction was right.

Area man or **Area woman**. Someone who is not a "local man" or "local woman" but who lives somewhere in the audience area. Georgia reporter Elizabeth Connor always wonders where the area starts and ends.

Arguably. Impossible to substantiate, as in: "He is arguably the best National League left-handed pitcher ever from Connecticut with three consonants in his middle name." Arguably gives reporters the freedom to draw conclusions they wouldn't dare on their own. No one wants to say "certainly" when such a useful fudge factor is available.

Articulate. Reporter's word for "said", as "articulating official policy." The source explained something in complete sentences, without "ya' know" or "I mean" or "uhh" after every two words.

As first reported. If it refers to another newspaper or TV station, it means "We got scooped." Otherwise, it becomes, "As we were first to report...."

Astir. Anything moving or waking up, from a village at dawn or an armed revolt. "Region astir as second Arab leader is toppled in two months," the *Wall St. Journal* reported Feb 12, 2011.

Astonishing emotional power. When a film is so described by a critic, it means, "Use that emotional power to get out of the theater fast," according to a Hollywood writer who prefers to remain anonymous.

At this point in time. Now. Useful on TV when one is filling extra seconds before a break.

Attendees. People attending something. Diana Dawson,

a former reporter who teaches journalism at the University of Texas, will toss a paper back to any student using the term.

Attributed. This refers to a quote the authenticity of which a reporter does not have the time to verify.

At the end of the day. The winner of the 2010 Trite Trophy, awarded by Gene Collier, of the *Pittsburgh Post-Gazette*, who writes: "It is likely the most ubiquitous cliché in the culture today, a cliché that simply 'Wouldn't Be Denied,' a cliché that simply 'Imposed Its Will' on the Trite. A ridiculous construction that has supplanted 'When It's All Said And Done' in the broader language, 'At The End Of The Day' easily meets the three ageless criteria for our annual championship: it's everywhere, it's essentially meaningless (very little of what follows 'At The End Of The Day' could not have been said without it) and I have to really, really hate it."

Authoritarian. The style with which dictators and tyrants rule.

Avid fan. A big-mouth who could drink beer through an entire game and still be able to shout blasphemies at the opposing team.

Award–winning journalist. One with a Pulitzer or other major award. DEEP TRANSLATION: Essayist John Leo pins this on "any reporter employed three or more years that still has a pulse."

B }

Backlog. That which happens to a caseload in courts. Any reporter knows that on a slow day a story can be patched together to fit the classic headline: "Judge Complains of Rising Case Backlog." See also *Logjam*.

Badly. People get badly injured, cars or houses badly damaged, but they are never injured or damaged nicely or well. "Badly" was once among words banned by copyeditors. Now copy editors have been replaced by bad spell-check software.

Bagging. As in "bagging their quarry," this means shooting animals in the wild. Other euphemisms: culling, harvesting, thinning. But one reader of *The Washington Post* complains about coverage of "macho psychotics who hide in the woods and slaughter defenseless animals."

Band-Aid solution. Used when a solution does not work because not enough money has been spent. If more money is spent, the requisite cliché is that the problem will not go away "by throwing money at it."

Baron. Any owner of a brewery carries the title of Baron. Gangster Dutch Shultz was the Beer Baron of the Bronx in the 1930s.

Barrel-chested. A top-heavy guy. Bodyguards, bouncers, football players, drill sergeants and basso profundo opera singers can fit this description. Only men are barrel-chested. Women's chests are rarely, if ever, described in media other than in "adult" and "men's" publications.

Based. Artists, actors, writers are always based someplace, such as "Miami-based." They rarely live in a city. Military personnel, however, are stationed at army, navy, air force or Marine bases, but are never based at bases.

Basically. Filler word, often heard on TV news, which is another way of saying essentially or mainly.

ABUNDANTLY OPENING WITH ADVERBS

"Basically, there is nothing wrong with initial adverbs except repeated over-use," wrote Fritz Spiegl, in *Keep Taking the Tabloids*, published in 1983. Naturally, his admonishment fell on the usual deaf ears. Not surprisingly, adverbial openers, most noticeably in TV news, still abound. Inspirationally, Mr. Spiegl gave this example of how the book of Genesis would be rewritten if Fleet Street edited it.

"INITIALLY, God created the heaven and the earth. BASICALLY, the earth was without form, and void. NOTICEABLY, darkness was upon the face of the deep. REPORTEDLY, the spirit of God moved upon the waters. LOFTILY, God said, Let there be light. PREDICTABY, there was light. BRILLIANTLY, God called the light Day and, ADDITIONALLY, the darkness he called Night. CURIOUSLY, God created Man in His own image...STARTINGLY, male and female created He them...THANKFULLY, God saw everything that He had made and, INTERESTINGLY, it was good. SUBSEQUENTLY, the evening and the morning were the sixth day...etc."

Basking in the glow. Smug.

Battle of the bulge. Obligatory description of people trying to lose weight. Commonly used after Thanksgiving, Christmas and New Year. "Portion Control Helps In Holiday Battle Of The Bulge," advised channel3000.com, of Madison, WI, on Nov. 24, 2011, adding, "Experts Warn Not To Skip Meals Over Thanksgiving Holiday." Most people under 60 have no idea what, where or when the original Battle of the Bulge was.

Bean counters. Accountants, bookkeepers, treasurers or the one who scrutinizes expense accounts. The *baristi* filling the coffee grinders at Starbucks are never bean counters since *contabile dei chichi de caffé* is too complicated Italian even for Starbucks.

Beautiful People. Plain folks with lots of money who spend more money on their hair than books, education, charity or the arts.

Behemoth. Adjective exclusively reserved for describing troubled nuclear or coal-fired power stations. "Seagull droppings cripple behemoth power plant."

Behind closed doors. As Joe Goulden explained in an email about this entry of what he terms Journo-Speak: "A not-so-subtle way of suggesting that the subject of a news story has something to hide, and thus is seeking seclusion away from prying eyes. A good example of using such wordage is when it's factually accurate, but contextually off-base. Consider this elbow-in-ribs writing in an article in *The New York Times* during the prolonged hearings into suspected wrongdoing by the Murdoch media empire in Britain: 'Mr. Murdoch has been in London since Thursday, conferring with a coterie of advisers, lawyers and communications consultants behind closed doors' (*NYT*, April 25, 2012, page one)." Perhaps *The Times* would have been happier had Mr. Murdoch chose to conduct his strategy session on the public green. It goes without saying that the decision to put the story on page one was made "at a meeting of top Times editors behind closed doors."

Beleaguered. Hounded by critics, most often in the media.

Bemused. The smile that secretly amused interviewees supposedly wear, except that the word actually means "muddled" or "stupefied."

Best movie of the year. Film reviewers' plaudit, even if it's only January, according to Marty Shindler, Los Angeles consultant.

Bewitched. Compulsory in every story about Halloween or Salem, Mass.

Bible-quoting. Prudish activist.

Biblical proportions. The writer doesn't really know exactly how big something is. Usually a natural disaster, like a flood or earthquake, and it's a combination of gigantic, huge, tremendous, humongous and big as all get-out.

GOSPEL JOURNALESE

If journalese is the language of reporting, there is no better early source—the Old and New Testaments. Donald Meyer, in *The Protestant Search for Political Realism*, 1919-1941, writes of rhetoric used in organizing early trade unions, and quotes T. B. Cowan, a Chattanooga Presbyterian: "...the Bible was still the best textbook for the labor firing line; Gospel journalese, with the fire of the prophets and the pointedness of Paul, was the language for popular prophetic preaching."

Harold Lohr, retired Lutheran Bishop, offering some examples of "early reporters" using Biblical journalese, quoted the British TV show *Beyond the Fringe*: "What are you guys doing out here on this cold winter night?" One answered, "We're abiding, man; we're abiding, keeping watch over our flocks by night." And: "A quick word in from the Jerusalem Gazette: Late last night, our reporter informs us, Zechariah begat Zephaniah."

A *Journalese* consultant theologian searched the Bible, the King James Version, first published in 1611, with the help of www. BlueLetterBible.org, and came up a long list of "Gospel Journalese" used repeatedly through the Bible, some words over 200 times. A word often associated with the Bible, "Apocalypse," is not found in the King James Version, while "Armageddon" is found only once. It is heart-warming to learn that several non-journalese words are far more plentiful than their violent journalese opposites: "peace" is found 429 times in 400 verses and "love" is found 311 times in 281 verses.

Here is a selection of a few Biblical "journalese" words, some still favorites of journalists.

Atone, Behemoth, Dirge, Epicurean, Exhort, Gird, Guile, Libertine, Loathsome, Loquacious, Panoply (meaning a full suit of armour, heavily armed), Perdition, Pernicious, Prodigal, Publican (a tax collector, and he wasn't running a pub), Ravenous (cruel, savage, vicious, and not just hungry for supper), Ruinous, Slay and Smite (both used early, in Genesis), Vengeance, Wax rich, Wax poor, Wrought ("What hath God wrought!" Frequently claimed as Alexander Graham Bell's comment when his assistant confirmed that Bell's first electrically transmitted message worked.)

Bildungsroman. Book reviewer shows off he wasn't entirely asleep in German 101. Reviewers who prefer plain English write, "coming of age."

Bilk. What swindlers do. Others steal.

Bitter. Damn cold. Heat is never bitter.

Blame. Something police, prosecutors, reporters say is the cause of something bad. Blame is usually laid on and if there is no question, blame is laid squarely on.

Blind eye. What is turned to illegal goings-on accepted by police, regulators, authorities, and others who get paid to enforce laws.

Blockbuster. A book, film, play, concert that has had big sales or audiences and the writer figures nobody will argue if it's described as such. Bombs are no longer called block-busters, even if today's are much more destructive than the originals in World War II, which could blow apart an apartment house, called a "block" in British English.

Blue Ribbon panel. A group of geezers, including at least one banker, a former politician, a retired judge, and a professor, none of whom have been recently indicted, and have nothing better to do. They are appointed by a governor or mayor who wants nothing done on something she or he wants everyone to forget about.

Body of a dead man. That which is found in "densely wooded areas." This is as opposed to "the body of a live man" which we never hear about.

Bold. Statements made by public figures that say something without the usual hedging.

Boldfacers. Entertainment writers' description of celebrities whose names are printed in bold-faced type in gossip columns.

Bombshell. Describes an event that the editor thinks may wake up a reader or two.

Boondoggle. Any public project that the paper doesn't approve. The *Boston Herald*, no fan of Boston's Big Dig, reported on May 24, 2011: "... a *Herald* review found widespread reports of cracks, leaks and deterioration that raise more questions about the safety of the scandal-plagued $15 billion boondoggle." If a paper does approve of a project, it's a long-awaited infrastructural necessity. See also *Widespread*, *Raise questions*, *Scandal-plagued*.

Bow out. What performers do when they retire or leave a job.

Boys of summer. Overworked collective description of baseball players often employed in stories in which they are portrayed as hapless lads. "Another glorious baseball season is upon us—ah, I can smell the sweet scent of money drifting through the morning haze—and my unlikely sympathies go out to the fans of New York, who are doubly taxed to help sustain the boys of summer." *The Washington Post*, Apr. 4, 2011.

Brace for. What people do when they are preparing for something bad, such as a storm, or unemployment report or traffic jams when a candidate running for president comes to town.

Brand. Business writers' way of describing a company, thus delighting and enriching ad agencies and PR consultants who charge clients big money for "corporate branding", which once was known as advertising and public relations.

Brash. Said of those who can only talk about themselves: egocentric.

Breakneck. Faster than high-speed. "Egypt geared up yesterday for a breakneck rush to democracy," the *Wall St. Journal* reported, Feb. 16, 2011.

Break-out performance. The first time on stage. Sometimes also the last time.

Breakthrough. A discovery the reporter never heard of and can't find quickly on the Web.

Breeze. This is how well-connected nominees are said to go through confirmation hearings.

Bristled. A politician's or businessman's reaction to a rare hardball question.

Brouhaha. A fight where words are thrown but no punches. The *Boston Herald*, in a business story on Sept 18, 2011, couldn't resist this groaner headline: "Brouhaha over 9/11 Bud ad — Hopped-up version of '02 tribute hard to swallow, says ad firm chief."

Brush with the law. What's on a rap sheet, usually in the plural, as "His former brushes with the law range from loud mufflers to attempted murder." Also something in the past of upper middle class citizens, as opposed to a poor person's "criminal history."

Brutal. Obligatory adjective to describe cold weather or dictatorships. Never used to describe hot weather or dictators the reporter wants to interview.

Bubbly. (1) A woman who smiles, laughs, jokes, calls reporters by their first names. Men are never bubbly. (2) Champagne.

Buff. A bore with focus. A person interested in something, such as the Civil War or the Great Wall of China, and will chew your ear off about it without prompting.

Buffet. When not referring to a piece of furniture or the Oracle of Omaha (who spells it Buffett), it's a battle or a storm. "Wind farm controversy buffets tiny Block Island," headlined theday.com, New London, CN, May 29, 2012.

Bulk up. Get fat.

Bunker. Any large reinforced concrete building where politicians or officials hunker down behind closed doors.

Burgeoning. Growing at a rate so fast the reporter can't be bothered to check exactly how fast.

Burly. At least 50 pounds overweight. All construction workers are burly even if they are short, skinny guys.

Burst on the scene. Performers making a professional debut. Authors burst on the literary scene, singers on the recording scene. They also take cities by storm.

But. Reporter gives himself or herself a way out: "Many agree with the governor, but some disagree."

Buttoned-down. Dull, dreary, boring. Washington is often described as "this buttoned-down town."

Buzz. A person mentioned it at the bar.

Byzantine. Proud description of every big city's political machinery.

Cachet. A person's personality. Reporter likes to sprinkle stories with foreign-sounding words, even though they are often misused, misspelled and mispronounced. See also *Schadenfreude*.

Calculus. Highfalutinese for figuring the odds. Political commentators love the word. "What the hell are you talking about?" a reporter who wrote "calculus" would ask if told the definition of "calculus of variations," as given in the *American Heritage Dictionary of the English Language*: "The mathematical analysis of the maxima and minima of definite integrals, the integrands of which are functions of independent variables, dependent variables and the derivatives of one or more dependent variables.". In an editorial about an earthquake in Kashmir, *The St. Louis Post-Dispatch*, Oct 12, 2005, figured: "In the calculus of horror, it falls somewhere between last December's Asian tsunami, which killed 232,000, and Hurricane Katrina, which killed about 1,200 people in Louisiana, Mississippi and Alabama."

Calloused hands. All blue collar workers' hands are calloused, even if reporters never saw them. "…. calloused hands of shipwrights

now long dead," wrote *The Washington Post*, Aug. 15, 2010, describing wooden remains of a ship built 200 years ago.

Cannot be ruled out. Term used with the highest grade of space-filling speculation. A longer way of saying, "But…"

Cantankerous. An old, cranky public official, usually male.

Card carrying. A solid supporter of something the reporter doesn't like, as a card carrying member of the NRA. People who belong to organizations the reporter likes do not carry cards, but are dedicated advocates.

Careen. What wayward planes do when they veer off a runway.

Caring. Not outwardly mean or rotten.

Cash-strapped. Usually, cities or towns going broke, but they also include states and entire nations: "Obama Signs $26 Billion Bailout for Cash-Strapped States," reported foxnews.com, Aug. 10, 2010. "Cash-strapped Belarus allows its currency to float," reported *The Miami Herald*, Apr. 19, 2011. Even ball clubs enjoy the title: "MLB loaned cash-strapped Mets $20M," headlined the *New York Post* Feb 25, 2011. And, of course, "Cash-strapped college kids find refuge in thrift stores," okgazette.com, Apr. 20, 2011. When it's a popular non-profit organization short of money, reporters rarely mention that the group pays no taxes and is run by well-paid executives. Millionaires and big-profit corporations are the only ones in the world that are not cash-strapped.

Caught up with. Indicates a reporter is out there doggedly chasing after an extremely busy person, who, in reality, is eager to be interviewed and get publicity. As in, "I caught up with Senator Bloviate...."

Cavernous. Any large factory or building, even if the reporter has never been in it. "Critics have long taken aim at food served in many of Boston's elementary school cafeterias: processed, frozen meals sealed in plastic and trucked hundreds of miles from cavernous factories far from New England," *The Boston Globe* reported May 31, 2011. However, small spaces can also be cavernous. *The Detroit Free Press*, Jan. 11, 2012, praised the "cavernous interior" of the Nissan eNV200 and on Feb 9, 2012, the "cavernous 15.2 cubic feet" of the Buick Verano's trunk. But in a *Free Press* story Dec.11, 2011, Ford planned to close a "sprawling, cavernous plant" in Minnesota. See also *Hulking*.

Caught flatfooted. A politician or executive didn't get his PR person to prepare an answer. Rarely used, however, for fear of rebuke by the National Association of Fallen Arches.

Celebrated. A person who once won an award. Wikipedia has a brief bio on them.

Chafe. Headlinese for irritate, annoy, bug the heck out of.

Charismatic. A big mouthed glad-hander.

Checkered past. Got caught playing around, and it wasn't checkers.

Challenged. Got a tough time handling something, as, "The vocabulary-challenged Boston Mayor Thomas Menino, who once described a nagging problem as 'an Alcatraz around my neck'."

Chattering classes. Pundits, columnists, academicians and other know-it-alls with opinions on everything. Not us, of course.

Chiseled. Describes the "features" of a man with a prominent nose, big chin, deep-set eyes, muscular body and a tough-guy look.

Claim. We don't believe what the person says, but here it is. A reporter who likes a source, never says he or she "claims" something. Instead, it's "firmly stated."

Claimed responsibility. Confessed to a crime, often a heinous one involving more than one death. "A terrorist group today claimed responsibility for taking the lives of 54 innocent people." Terrorists also "execute" their victims, while garden variety thugs "murder" them. *Factiva*, the Dow-Jones collection of news sources, reports 105,445 stories with "claimed responsibility", as of mid-April, 2011.

Classic. Something the reporter remembered seeing or hearing someplace.

Claw back. Politicians pledge to get back public money stolen by contractors or suppliers or other crooks. Usually, the Attorney General or other agency is declawed by the crooks' far smarter lawyers. Fritz Spiegl, British authority on journalist jargon, explained in *Keep Taking the Tabloids*, published in 1983: "The Lord giveth and the Lord taketh away...but the government gives and then claws back what it can." The term was proudly used by state or federal agencies to show they were recovering a bit of the billions of taxpayer money handed out to rescue or subsidize failing financial institutions or corporations.

Closely watched. Something so closely watched you have to be reminded it is being closely watched. The reporter accidentally spotted online that there was a development in a story most people never heard of.

Clout. What powerhouses and insiders have plenty of.

Cobblestones. All quaint towns or neighborhoods are paved with cobblestones, even if they are not. "Boston's cobblestone streets aren't great for modern traffic, but they add to the romance of older neighborhoods like the North End," was the cutline of a photo in a USA Today travel piece. The photo showed Acorn St., on Beacon Hill, a long way from the North End, which has no streets paved with cobblestones.

Co-conspirator. Conspirator.

Coffers. The pot of money, usually the government's. Amy Menefee Payne, director of communications of Americans for Prosperity, says, "This is used often by statehouse reporters who are writing their 47th budget story of the month." Also a bank account. British journalist Graeme Whitfield in his Journalese-English Dictionary (first edition) says that no one—even a journalist—would say he was depositing a check into his coffers.

Collision course. This is what opposing sides are always on.

Come forward. What TV reporters say police want witnesses or informants to do.

Coming of age. Term used when a newspaper has finally gotten around to writing about a subject but has no news lead for it except for the vague notion that it has come of age. "Woolen mittens come of age," for instance. Also, a description of any book or movie about teen-agers trying to get laid.

Coming to terms with. Said of school children after a senseless shooting or family members after a tragedy. Regardless of what sort of counseling is being offered, the news story must say that the survivors were struggling to come to terms with it. Also, learning to cope.

Coming up. TV newscaster's tickler of hot stories, hoping viewers won't switch channels while commercials run. "And coming up. Nor'easter to wallop coast with one millimeter of rain; Tiger Woods' comeback—Can he get his putts under control? And World War Three breaks out. Coming up. Be right back."

Companion. Someone much closer than a person he or she simply liked to take a walk with.

Compelling. Book reviewer already used "Riveting."

Competorize. To make something competitive.

Complex. A building project with at least two different occupants, such as apartments and retail space. Also, any government or business scheme the reporter can't figure out.

Compulsive. Book reviewer favorite when riveting, compelling or gripping has already been used.

Concerned. Somebody's worried. Vince Filak found that concerned citizens are usually loud people who showed up at something.

Concerns. When not referring to companies, it means worries, ranging from red tide's hurting Maine clam beds to Pakistan's nuclear weapons falling into Taliban hands.

Conflict of interest. Nice way of saying, "This really stinks but no indictments have been issued."

Confrontation. Any conflict, from a shouting match to guys shooting at each other.

Considered. The reporter says the subject is something. Most often written as "widely considered" which means the editor agrees. Consider yourself a boob if you didn't know that "The Fat Duck, a restaurant to the west of London, is widely considered one of the world's finest cathedrals to modernist cuisine...," according to Sam Sifton of *The New York Times*, May 24, 2011. See also **Many** and *Some say*.

Content. Stuff on webpages. Tim Rutten, columnist for the *Los Angeles Times*, commenting on Feb. 9, 2011, about AOL's acquisition of the Huffington Post, explains that "content is what journalism becomes when it's adulterated into a mere commodity."

Continued to search. Third-day follow-up to a crime story. Whether or not any searching is going on, it is safe for the media to assume it's what the cops are doing, even if they haven't a clue.

Convivial. Drunken and debauched. As in, "The ex-boyfriend of the bride enjoyed himself at the reception, and contributed to the convivial atmosphere."

Cornerstone. When not something the Mayor lays for a building, it's a key piece of a project, plan or scheme.

Correspondent. A fancier title for a free-lancer or stringer, usually paid by the word, story, or time.

Countless thousands. A helluva lot. There were "countless thousands" of demonstrators in Cairo, according to *ABC-TV* reporter Terry Moran, Feb 8, 2011, who evidently saw so many he lost count.

Courage. Universal attribute of people with problems who have not attempted suicide. Also used to describe movie and rock stars that have persisted in the face of minor setbacks. "Despite a failed face-lift and bust enhancement, and the onset of middle age, she mustered the courage to continue her career as a belly dancer."

Courtesy of or **In cooperation with**. NPR and PBS code words for commercials, which are instead announced as "sponsored by...".

CQ. JOURNOSPEAK to indicate in a written text that something is correct no matter how goofy it sounds. Also (*sic*).

Craggy. Said of a face that would stop a clock.

Crippled. A ship with a hole in it or any large plant or project with serious problems, such as the "crippled BP oil well in the Mexican Gulf."

Crippling. Blows that struggling companies or projects are hit with. Snowstorms or floods always cripple traffic.

Crisis. Whatever the latest problem that's worthy of a story, and which the reporter says is a crisis. Crises can range from bedbugs invading a posh hotel in Manhattan to zebras not reproducing fast enough in Tanzania. A "political crisis" can range from an armed revolt to a top politician's spending taxpayer money on a fact-finding mission to St. Bart's with his 20-year-old blonde "expert international trade consultant."

Critics' pick. They picked it as the worst of the week or month, but that's not what the promotion material says.

Crucial. Reporter impresses readers of the vital importance of what he or she is covering. Countries that are dubious friends of the U.S. can suddenly become crucial, as

The New York Times reported on rioting in Cairo, Jan 26, 2011: "The burst of civil unrest appeared to threaten the stability of a crucial Arab ally of the United States."

Crossroads. Where all governmental bodies are after paying consultants to tell them what is going wrong.

Crunch. This applies to money and oil when there seems to be a shortage, even though it may be a glut. It becomes "crunch time" when making a decision on an important matter can no longer be avoided. Accountants, analysts and economic forecasters crunch numbers. Other people simply make calculations.

Crushing. Any defeat whether it's by one point in a basketball game or 100 votes in a Senate election.

Crusty. Old and obnoxious.

Cycle of violence. At least two crimes in two days.

Cultivated. A gentleman who doesn't use the F-word too often when women and children are around, at least not when he's sober. Ladies are always cultivated, no matter what they say.

Cure-all. See *Panacea*.

Cushy. Usually a public job that pays better than the reporter's.

Curiosity delays. Traffic reporter code for the rubbernecks slowing down to try to catch a glimpse of the carnage.

Curious. Nosy as hell.

Czar. A civil servant or politician put in charge of something and having responsibilities that the reporter or editors don't like.

Dampen. Rain never dampens spirits at an outdoor party, wedding, fiesta, or PR event. "Rain shortens 787 first flight, fails to dampen optimism," cheered the Dec 16, 2009, *Seattle Times*. Nor can rain put out a fire, as the *Chicago Tribune* reported on May 14, 2011: "Rain can't dampen fire of 'Idol' contender's hometown fans." However, an accident or catastrophe, no matter in what form, can. "Drought dampens hopes of wildlife survival," headlined yourhoustonnews.com, Oct. 22, 2011, and in China, "Tax burden dampens entrepreneurs," headed a story in globaltimes.cn, on Oct. 19, 2011.

Darker corners of the mind. Obligatory cliché in stories about poets, who, of course, are serious poets. "In her poems about jack-o-lanterns, she explores the darker corners of the mind." A favorite in NPR reviews.

Date with. A Nobel Prize winner has a date with destiny; a space probe has a date with a far distance planet, at least when it doesn't have a rendezvous with it; a presidential candidate has a date with history.

Death toll. "Never a count. Or a number. Never written or uttered outside of the news, either," wrote Frank Fellone of *The Arkansas Democrat-Gazette*.

Decades-old. The reporter couldn't quickly find the date online but remembered granddad talking about it. *The Seattle Times* on Jan 26, 2012, ran a Reuters story reporting that Alaska Airlines announced it would end "a decades-old tradition of handing out prayer cards with its in-flight meals."

Decorated. Any veteran who was awarded at least a Good Conduct Ribbon.

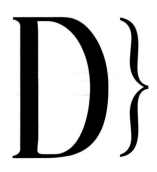

Deep pockets. Rich. Someone with deep pockets usually has plenty of clout.

Defining. A moment or event that the reporter must inflate since he's writing about it. See also *Telling*.

Defunct. Went bankrupt, went out of business, kaput.

Delicate. A landscape in which all controversial projects are proposed.

Demand answers. What reporters say the public demands after a major bureaucratic screw-up. The demands are usually forgotten in a couple of days. No answers are given.

Densely-wooded area. Where most badly decomposed bodies are found. Also a target for small planes in trouble. See also *Body of a dead man*, which is found in these areas.

Deny. What politicians and business leaders do automatically when confronted with something they definitely do not want to be confronted with.

Devastating. A military offensive against an enemy the reporter and the paper are rooting for. If they don't like the enemy, it's a successful military offensive.

Developing nation. It has a legitimate use but sometimes has to be understood in DEEP TRANSLATION: A poverty-stricken country, usually run by a dictator, which has not developed into anything for as long as anyone can remember.

Device. Any explosive or bomb. Tom Lehrer, in his classic 1965 album *That was the Year That Was*, introduced his song, "Who's Next?" by using the term in an early meaning, saying: "One of the big news items of the past year concerned the fact that China, which we called 'Red China', exploded a nuclear bomb, which we called a device. Then Indonesia announced that it was going to have one soon, and proliferation became the word of the day." A device can now also be a smartphone, iPad, Kindle or any other high-tech gadget.

Dialogue. As a verb, contributor Samantha Friedman, of Washington, DC, explains it's what mayors say they'll do about something, as, "I will dialogue with citizens about what they want to see happen." Usually it will be a mayoral monologue.

Did not return phone calls. A public figure who has just been indicted is not only guilty but hiding.

Dignitary. Anyone with a title in front of his or her name, or letters after it.

Dire. In really bad trouble. Straits are always dire, even if those reported to be in dire straits have never been closer to a strait than up the creek without a paddle.

Disabled. Only cars or trucks are disabled, causing traffic jams. People are no longer disabled or handicapped.

Disastrous. A real big screw-up that reporters remember. As Holly Robichaud explained in the *Boston Herald*, Feb. 14, 2011, "The key to the event are the speeches. One bad address can be a dream killer. Just ask Louisiana Gov. Bobby Jindal, who is still trying to recover from his disastrous State of the Union response two years ago."

Docu-drama. Work of televised or cinematic fiction about a famous person. Also called a Biopic.

Documents. Financial transactions of an intricate nature submitted in a court case. As defined by Joe Goulden, "A bunch of paper (contracts, debentures, deeds of sale, etc.) introduced into court which the reporter (a) could not understand and (b) could not find a lawyer willing to give him a fast short-course."

Dog. Bother, trouble, worry. A politician is always dogged by an old scandal, indictment or conviction.

Dogged. A nuisance with a cause.

Don. Any boss of the Mafia, when he is not a capo. Dons are always refuted or alleged.

Down the block. Where politicians like to send their opponents.

Draconian. Term that first got widespread press use in the 1980s describing the Gramm-Rudman deficit-reduction law. The adjective, for that which is cruel or exceedingly harsh, comes from Draco, a legislator of ancient Athens. "Draco," wrote William Power in *The Wall Street Journal*, "seems to get more press some days than Sen. Ernest Hollings, the law's third sponsor." Since then, the proliferation of the term is such that a January 2011 search of Google News came up with 1,441 news stories in which the term was used.

Dramatic. So exciting or earth-shaking that you forgot all about it until the reporter reminded you. "It's a word we use when we're pushing too hard," wrote Mike Feinsilber, AP writing coach, in a memo.

Draw Fire. When not referring to bullets, what politicians get from angry activists.

Dreaded. Everything the reporter doesn't like, from taxes to speed traps to a dictator's security police. Howie Carr, *Boston Herald* columnist, when writing about hacks' political jobs, always refers to the alternative as "the dreaded private sector."

Droves. What more than a dozen people flee or arrive in.

Duke it out. Fight. "Look-alike 'critter' wines duke it out," headlined a story in *The Wall Street Journal,* Feb 25, 2011, about cheap wines with all kinds of animals on the label. Only reporters over 70, or fans of 1930s tough guy films, would use the expression, "Put up your dukes." If still in use, it would be politically correct to say, "Put up your Duchesses" if addressing a lady.

Dues. What politicians, athletes, executives have paid to get where they are, as, "He paid his dues as the Governor's chauffeur before being named chief of protocol."

Dynamic. When it doesn't describe a powerful athlete or sports team, it means all kinds of things are going on. As *The Baltimore Sun* reported, Dec. 5, 2009, "...still, experts in jury *dynamics* said the undisclosed history is enough for the mayor's defense attorneys to ask that the jury's verdict be thrown out."

Easy answers. There are never any of these. See also *Panacea*.

Ebullient. Crazy; off the wall.

Eccentric. If a person is a wacko, a screwball, or just plain nuts, he or she is eccentric if the person is also rich.

Eerily. Streets that are dark or deserted are always eerily silent.

800-pound gorilla. One huge something. Illustrations of 800-pound gorillas are Microsoft, Google and Facebook. Gorillas relegated to the primate old-age home include General Electric, IBM and Kodak. The gorilla has put on weight over the years, starting at 600 pounds, then 700, and even 1,000, 2,000, and up to 10,000 pounds. But 800 is the favorite, getting most hits, about 536,000, in a Google search in early 2012. The suggested origin is in an old riddle: "Where does an 800 lb. gorilla sleep?" The answer: "Anywhere it wants to."

Elderly. Anyone older than the reporter's father or mother.

ELECTION JOURNALESE

Mike Feinsilber of the AP created this conversation some years ago, but it still works in an era when the primary season is now three times longer.

Q. Did the candidate campaign in Ohio?
A. No. He took his campaign to the Buckeye State.
Q. Then what did he do?
A. He criss-crossed the state.
Q. Is that all?
A. Sometimes he zig-zagged across the state.
Q. How would you characterize the state?
A. It is a key battleground.
Q. What did the candidate do when met by a big crowd at the airport?
A. Sometimes he pressed the flesh. Other times he worked the ropeline.
Q. What did he propose to solve a problem?
A. A 10-point program. (Headline writers rejoice at that; readers shrug.)
Q. Is the candidate confident?
A. He is buoyed by the polls.
Q. Nonetheless...
A. He will take nothing for granted.
Q. So what does his opponent face?
A. He faces an uphill battle.
Q. So what does he do over the weekend?
A. He huddles with advisers.
Q. And if he does it in midweek?
A. He breaks off campaigning to hole up with advisers.
Q. Just any old advisers?
A. No. With key advisers. Sometimes top advisers.
Q. What if the leader exaggerates his opponent's advantages?
A. He's playing the expectations game.

Q. One candidate has lots of money.
A. He amassed a campaign war chest.
Q. What does the frontrunner remind the voters?
A. That every vote counts.
Q. And his opponent?
A. That the only vote that counts occurs on Election Day.
Q. What did the candidates do in the hours before Election Day?
A. They sprinted to the finish line.
Q. What about seats that are open?
A. They are up for grabs.
Q. It looks like a close election.
A. It is down to the wire.
Q. In that case?
A. It promises to be a long night.
Q. And the voters?
A. They went to the polls in droves.
Q. Is that all?
A. No, they trooped to the polls.
Q. Before the results are known, where was the candidate?
A. He holed up in a hotel.

Eleventh hour. When reprieves arrive on death row and when strikes are averted "after marathon bargaining sessions."

Elite. Any third world army unit that has polished boots and can march in step. Also a police unit that have more and bigger guns and gadgets than ordinary cops carry.

THE ELONGATED YELLOW FRUIT SYNDROME

In his caustic remarks in *The Arkansas Democrat-Gazette*, editor Frank Fallone identified this as a phenomenon closely related to journalese. He defines it as "the overpowering urge, when writing about bananas, not to use the same word more than once in close proximity; thus on second reference, never banana, but an elongated yellow fruit.

This syndrome was noted by John Leo in his first essay on Journalese in *Time*: "The discipline required for a winter storm report is awesome. The first reference to seasonal precipitation is 'snow,' followed by 'the white stuff,' then either 'it' or 'the flakes,' but not both. The word snow may be used once again toward the end of the report, directly after discussion of ice-slicked roads and the grim highway toll."

The late Colonel Moammar al-Gaddafi, whose name is spelled by the media in dozens of ways (*ABC News* found 122 different spellings) provides reporters and editors with a long choice of descriptions for the guy, to avoid repeating his name, however it is spelled. "Libyan leader" is the mildest description, as in *The New York Times* story, Apr. 23, 2011: "The search for a country to accept Khadafy has been conducted quietly....even though the Libyan leader has shown defiance in recent days...." In the previous sentence of the story, he was identified as "the dictator." Other media descriptions, in various publications, include: strongman, longtime Libyan personality, tyrant, murderous tyrant, mad dog, erratic, bizarre, ruler of a kleptocracy.

Embattled. The term applied to almost anyone or anything that is under attack, and generally when it's the media doing the attacking. "Embattled is one of those funny words seldom used outside a daily newspaper," wrote Mike Berry of the *Orlando Sentinel*, "I doubt I would ever hold the following conversation with a friend: "So, how's your wife doing these days?" "Embattled, now that you ask."

Emotional. Required adjective for "reunion" and "home-coming."

End of an era. When a politician most people have never heard of and don't give two hoots about retires or goes to jail. Also when an obsolete product is taken off the shelves or when a soap opera is cancelled on TV. New eras always dawn.

Engaging. Reviewer's standby for a book that's OK, but not riveting or compelling.

Engineering marvel. Any public construction job a paper supports that's more complicated than filling a pot-hole. Boston's Big Dig was often described as such in *Boston Globe* news stories until a woman was killed when a tunnel roof panel fell on her car.

Engulf. Covers anything from a fire to a hot protest over potholes.

Enshrined. Fancy way of describing a respected or historic law or custom. Halls of Fame enshrine people.

Ensnared. Tangled or trapped in something, often affecting politicians.

Epic. Something huge or amazing, often in epic proportions. The 60-mile-long traffic jam in China in August, 2010, was "epic" and will remain so until an even bigger jam occurs.

Epicenter. A favorite term for the center of anything, not just earthquakes. CBS, on Dec. 15, 1992, used it in reference to both Los Angeles riots and starvation in Somalia.

Epidemic. A noticeable trend. A journalese classic was when major networks and news magazines discovered a "drug epidemic" in 1986 even though studies showed that drug use was on the decline. Said *Newsweek*, June 16: "An epidemic is abroad in America, as pervasive and as dangerous in its way as the plagues of medieval times." *Time* declared that as a result of the drug epidemic, fear "has seized the nation."

Equation. Something consisting of two equal parts. Unless he or she has kids in middle school, the reporter does not remember how to solve an algebraic equation.

Escalate. Increase. Get bigger. Get tougher.

Eschew. To avoid or shun. Used by reporters and editors who like to show they were not asleep in Shakespeare 101, and remember Falstaff's admonition: "What cannot be eschew'd must be embraced."

Essentially. Choice TV news term meaning absolutely nothing, although the reporter may think it's important. "The highway crash has essentially blocked the highway."

Estimated at. Reporters accept without question crowd sizes provided by officials, organizers, police or flacks, who exaggerate or diminish numbers to suit their agendas. The Boston media, for example, reported that one million Bruins fans cheered the Stanley Cup winners along a one-mile victory parade on

Facing up to.... The number of years, usually in the hundreds, a person on trial can get in prison if found guilty of all charges and gets sentenced the maximum on all, to be served "on and after". Usually applied to white collar criminals. Rarely does the story mention that the accused is most likely to plea bargain. He or she will end up with 12 months suspended, and two months community service.

Fall from grace. He or she got caught.

Famed. Someone or something so well-known that the reporter feels obliged to tell readers that the subject is famous, which they already know. "If something really is," asks the AP's Mike Feinsilber," why do we have to say so?" See *Well-known.*

Famously. An adverb used to show off a reporter's knowledge of something said or written that is so well known it's famous. The *San Francisco Chronicle* reported Feb. 2, 2012, "F. Scott Fitzgerald famously said that there are no second acts in American life—an adage that is usually cited only in order to refute it. Now *The Great Gatsby* is poised to offer the latest counterexample to the rule."

Fault-line. Political reporter's prediction of the point or issue on which politicians insist they won't budge their position. But they usually do.

Fears. The reporter is worried. "...renewing fears of a second recession."

Fearsome. Scary.

Feeding program. Serving the homeless. "They're people, not animals, for heavens sake," says contributor Cathy Boyd, of Austin, Texas.

Feeling the heat. Someone in big trouble.

Feisty. Belligerent. Always applied to lively, energetic women who berate public officials and call reporters and point out inaccuracies. Somehow, a man is never feisty, unless the story points out that he is no taller than 5'1".

Fete. Handy in headlines for a bash. When someone is feted, he or she is honored.

FICTION, JOURNALESE IN

In *The Imperfectionists* (Dial Press, New York, 2010), Tom Rachman, who worked as an AP reporter and an editor at the *International Herald Tribune*, writes: "Leo, the Rome correspondent for a Chicago newspaper, had mastered every cliché, his pieces unfolding in that journalese realm where refugees are endlessly flooding across borders, cities bracing for storms, voters heading for polls."

Edna Buchanan, in *Miami, It's Murder*. (Hyperion, 1994), has it down pat: "When I finally slept, I dream in headlines and bad newspeak: Predawn fires ... shark-infested waters ... steamy tropical jungles .... the solid South ... mean streets

and densely wooded areas populated by ever-present lone gunmen, fiery Cuban, deranged Vietnam veteran, Panamanian strongman, fugitive financier, bearded dictator, slain civil rights leader, grieving widow, struggling quarterback, cocaine kingpin, drug lord, troubled youth, embattled mayor, totally destroyed by, Miami-based, bullet-riddled, high-speed chase, uncertain futures, deepening political crises sparked by massive blasts, brutal murders, badly decomposed, benign neglect and blunt trauma.
"I woke up, nursing a dull headache."

In his 2009 novel, *Stone's Fall* (Spiegel & Grau, New York), Ian Pears, a one-time Brit journalist, has his writer character comment on an obituary of a financier he is investigating:

"As in most obituaries, the author said little about the man; they rarely do. But the reticence here was greater than usual. It mentioned that Ravenscliff left a wife, but did not say when they married. It said nothing at all about his life, nor where he lived. There were not even any of the usual phrases to give a slight hint: 'a natural raconteur' (loved the sound of his own voice); 'noted for his generosity to friends' (proliferate); 'a formidable enemy' (a brute); 'a severe but fair employer' (a slave-driver); 'devoted to the turf' (never read a book in his life); 'a life-long bachelor' (vice); 'a collector of flowers'—this meant a great womanizer. Why it came to mean such a thing I do not know."

James Aldridge, author and former Australian foreign correspondent, in his 1950 novel

The Diplomat, described the role of the press in post-war British Mid-East politics. It still applies. "He might have known that a good newspaper was supposed to present a cold statement of events with a fair balance of opposing opinions, but MacGregor had seen time and time again a serious moment in history treated as an amusing incident or a bright side-line to one man's embarrassment or another man's stupidity .... Newspapers were newspapers. You bought them for a penny and you read ... what unseen reporters said and you threw them the Thames when they annoyed you."

Fierce. When a clash gets serious.

Fiercely independent. A descriptive term that might as well be required by law to appear at least once in any personality profile of a politician or group of people who resist outside authority. The fiercely independent subject has, invariably "paid his/her dues."

Fighter. A guy with a Kalashnikov or rocket launcher, usually admired as long as he doesn't aim at the reporter.

Financially-plagued/financially-troubled. In debt; books don't balance. They were the two most popular hyphenated modifiers of the 1980s according to John Leo in his 1986 essay "Journalese: a Ground-Breaking Study."

Find closure/seek closure. What people who have been hit with a tragedy want .

Fine. Reviewer's shorthand for "I like this book, play or performance, although it wasn't exactly sizzling."

Finish each other's sentences. Husband and wife continually interrupt each other.

Firebrand. A wild, loud-mouthed activist, often a preacher.

Fire off. A letter or reply that is sent within a week or two.

Firestorm. At least two people protest or complain.

Firm. Applied to anyone whose politics the journalist likes. See also **Hard-line**.

Flailing. In big trouble, although the dictionary definition means threshing something with a flail. Sounds more impressive than floundering. "A year after Hewlett-Packard Co. purchased flailing Palm, the technology behemoth is rolling out the tablet using Palm's webOS operating system..." reported the *Los Angeles Times*, July 8, 2011.

Flack. Journalist slang for a public relations spokesperson for a politician or company. Never used in a story, however. Disrespecting a flack in print or on the air doesn't win drinks at the press club bar. Flak is what flacks produce.

Flamboyant. Ostentatious but in **DEEP TRANSLATION**: As John Leo defined it in *Time* in 1986: "familiar journalese word meaning 'kinky' or 'one who does not have all of his or her paddles in the water'."

Flatline. Something dies. "Ex-hospital Big's marriage flatlines," was a *Boston Herald* gossip column headline, Mar. 22, 2011. Never used flippantly about a real heart monitor flatline.

Flawed. Used by critics in reviews of films, plays, books, or whatever they may have thoroughly enjoyed but feel compelled to say something negative lest their editor thinks they have gone soft in the head and it's time for them to be assigned to covering zoning variance hearings. "Though flawed, it is the best daytime game show to debut this season."

Fledgling. A young and inexperienced person, but often used by fledgling reporters to mean faltering.

Flood tide. What red ink always flows in.

Flurry. When not snow, a lot of sudden activity, as a flurry of phone calls between the White House and the head of a country in a crisis.

Footage. Part of a video or film, even though it's all digital and there isn't even an inch of film, no less a foot.

Foreign article. Something that doesn't belong where it's found, like a frog in a bag of potato chips. Not to be confused with a story in a newspaper outside the country, or an article such as le, la, il, el, los, der, den and others you've forgotten from high school language classes.

Forensic. Obligatory adjective for any investigation involving a microscope and computer. Prior to TV show *CSI* and its spin-offs becoming popular, this was called searching for clues and evidence that would stand up in court.

Forthwith. Editorial writers' favorite admonition meaning now.

FOURTH ESTATE TITLES

"One of my duties as a United Press International correspondent in Memphis, Tenn., was to follow the escapades of Jerry Lee Lewis," wrote Mike Berry in *The Orlando Sentinel.*

"My first year on the job Lewis entered a Memphis hospital with bleeding ulcers. I wrote, rather mundanely, something to the effect of: singer Jerry Lee Lewis will undergo surgery today for . . .

"A more experienced reporter reviewing my copy explained that it needed some juicing up and changed that to piano-pounding entertainer Jerry Lee Lewis.

"Later I leafed through a clip file and discovered that, sure enough, Lewis's name was almost always preceded by the compound adjective piano-pounding entertainer.

"From then on I, too, referred to him by his Fourth Estate title. It's the price tag a reporter has to pay."
—Mike Berry. "Life Is A Cliché: A No-Win Situation, An Uphill Battle That Sounds The Alarm For A Wake-Up Call (If You Know What We Mean)," *The Orlando Sentinel*, Dec. 11, 1994.

Fracas. Fight but commonly a noisy fight outside a bar. The joke goes: "Was he punched in the fracas?" "No, in the jaw."

Fragile. All shorelines affected by an oil spill are fragile. Unless they are sensitive. Or precious.

Frantic search. The kind of search that people conduct when children are missing. A level-headed search won't do.

Fray. What happens when friendships or relations sour.

Free-wheeling. Chaotic; confused. "In a free-wheeling interview, the candidate lashed out against the Kremlin, frequent flier programs, diet colas, supermarket shopping carts with defective wheels, and the arms race."

Frenzy. At least three guys arguing.

Front and center. Get out in front. Only reporters who have been in the military know what this really means.

Fueled. What got the fight going, as jealousy-fueled, alcohol-fueled, rivalry-fueled.

Fundamental. That which affects the press. A line like, "The issue posed is fundamental" is invariably followed by a discussion of freedom of the press, censorship or copyright.

Fundamentally. The writer tells you in one short sentence what the two-column story or two-minute TV news report is all about. "The issue is fundamentally whether the mayor is on the take."

Further studies are needed. Obligatory closing in stories about new drugs or treatments being tested, as reported in a medical journal. See also *Suggested.*

Fury. Mild annoyance, "which a journalist has to flame up to get his story onto the front page," according Graeme Whitfield in thelatest.com blog "Six post office branches will be closed in Waltham Forest under plans announced this week, to the fury of customers and staff," as reported in *This is London,* February 19, 2011. Whitfield adds: "As it would never be said in real life: 'The corner shop has sold out of Mars bars. I react with fury'."

Game changer. Something big happened. "The American deaths were a game changer in the world of piracy," reported the AP, Mar 2, 2011, in a story about Somali pirates who don't play games.

Gaming. Euphemism for gambling. Used by papers supporting a casino. A specific lottery is always a "game". The effect is to make high-stakes gambling sound like Scrabble or Monopoly.

Gangland-style. Term for murders that involve one or more of the following elements: 1. a late-model car, 2. a victim seated in a barber chair, 3. a victim eating in an Italian restaurant, 4. gunmen wearing suits and shined shoes.

Garner. "Gather ye rosebuds, but please don't garner them," writes Frank Fellone in *The Arkansas Democrat-Gazette*. "Always makes me think of Garner Ted Armstrong, the radio evangelist of years past. Awards tend to be garnered. But no kid ever says, 'I garnered first place in the spelling bee, Mommy!'"

Gear up. To get something going. Gearing down would mean getting more muscle, if it were a car, which is where the expression probably originated, but reporters who have never driven a stick-shift car use "gearing down" to mean slowing down.

Genteel. Description of any refined, polite, older woman, no matter how feisty. If a woman's art exhibition is insufficiently strident it is genteel.

Gentleman. Cop-speak for a man who is not in uniform. "The gentleman was arrested for mugging two elderly ladies."

Get on board. Reporter has a boat and loves nautical terms. "So many people and organizations are getting on board, I sometimes fear

for their ability to remain afloat," comments Stanley Bloom, former radio reporter, of Stockholm, Sweden.

Gifted. Anyone who can walk and chew gum at the same time. Never used to describe a politician because they'd sue the paper for claiming he or she was on the take.

Gin up. When not referring to a Martini, it means promote, push, get started. "Designers gin up fashions with less cotton," headlined the *New York Post*, Mar. 23, 2001, with a pun only southerners would immediately catch.

Glass and concrete. Words used to show a writer's contempt for a building. "She went to work each morning at 9:00 in a soulless glass and concrete box."

Glitch. A screw-up worse than a hiccup.

Glittering. Casinos, theaters and other joints the reporter thinks are low-class. But in arts stories, they are high class.

Go for the jugular. Getting right to the point.

Go north / Head north. Prices climb.

Go south / Head south. Something drops or disappears. "Take my word for it." Mike Feinsilber wrote, "Southerners object to this way of saying something turned out bad. Went missing is equally tired, equally tiresome."

Gold standard. Hot stuff. Reporter doesn't know America went off the gold standard in 1933.

Golden opportunity. Reporter predicts it's going to be great.

Golf ball. Unit of measurement for hailstones.

Graffiti-marred neighborhood. A slum.

Graft ridden. A public office or agency where more than one bribe, pay-off or other shady activity has been exposed.

Grand illusion. The reporter was awake in Film Studies 101 when they showed *Grand Illusion,* the 1937 film about World War I. It's never used to describe war, but instead for such things as politicians' schemes for monstrous public projects that are never started and the paper opposed. Grand illusions are far bigger than plain old illusions, which are always shattered. See also *Illusions* and *Shattered.*)

Grandmother. Description of all women old enough to amaze reporters with the fact that the woman's children also has children. She is usually a grandmother of two or three or more, who sits in her immaculate avocado-green living room while being interviewed.

Gravitas. Latin for gravity. **DEEP TRANSLATION:** Qualities of a never-smiling bore.

Gravy train. The favored means of transportation for the well-connected. One of the few dozen terms cited in the *Reuters*

Handbook of Journalism as avoidable journalese.

Green. Anything a reporter figures is good for the environment, climate, health, humanity and the globe. Term formerly meant money. When it comes to heavily subsidized "green" projects it still means money.

Green light. Shopworn metaphor for an approval. In the *Reuters Handbook of Journalism,* green light gets a red light.

Grimy. Adjective for any small Midwestern city that once made steel or burned coal and does not have at least one good expense account restaurant.

Gripping. Book reviewer favorite when riveting or compulsive has already been used.

Grisly. Reporter looked at the scene and threw up.

Gritty. A slum. Also, a description of a plucky person over fifty who fights for a cause the reporter likes.

Grapple with. Politicians and bureaucrats always grapple with problems. They often lose the wrestling match.

Gray. All men older than the reporter's dad are gray-haired or graying. Older women are rarely described this way.

Grievously. A wound or injury causing even more grief, pain or anguish than a serious wound or injury.

Ground zero. A place where something big happens, as Tahrir Square in Cairo or the protest area at the capitol in Madison, Wisconsin were in 2011.

Growing evidence. The cops found more guns, dope and cash.

Grueling. Anything drawn-out, such as a trial or school-board meeting that the reporter has had the bad luck of being assigned to cover. Reporters also feel obliged to inform you, since you don't know it, that winter weather, floods, storms or other rough stuff are not pleasant.

Gubernatorial contest. Governor's race. "No ordinary citizen, but only writers of journalese prose, ever used the term 'gubernatorial contest.' Ordinary people said, 'the governor's race,'" is how Gilbert Moore put it in his collection of "bad newspaper writing." Moore added: "Gubernate. What, presumably, a successful gubernatorial candidate did after taking office, at least according to the late Ralph Storey of the CBS TV affiliate in Los Angeles. A wonderful word." In his 2001 essay on journalese in the *Bangor Daily News,* Richard Dudman cited gubernatorial as a prime example of journalese, adding that the word always sounded to him like a "peanut in a swimming pool."

Gushed. Reporter got tired of writing, "She said..."

Guru. Any authority who has not made an ass of himself in the last six months, or, in the case of financial gurus, the last two weeks. Seldom, if ever, applied to Indian wise men.

Gyrating. How the stock market moves.

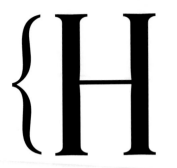{H

Hack. A politically-appointed civil servant or politician the reporter, editor or columnist doesn't like. The person who does the columnist a favor at City Hall is never a hack, at least not in print. A hack is also a reporter working for the opposition paper or TV station.

Hail of bullets. What gangsters often go down in. A lot of shots were fired and the reporter doesn't know how many.

Hallmark. A sign, logo or style, as "Senator Bloviate, puffing his hallmark Cohiba..."

Hamlet. A quaint term for what is supposed to be a quiet rural town. Not to be confused with the hero of the Shakespeare tragedy. *The Fort Worth Star-Telegram* on Jan 31, 2012, reporting about the town of Burleson, wrote that "a second high school was needed when the longtime farming and livestock hamlet south of Fort Worth found itself with a surplus of people instead of crops."

Hammer. What storms do to coasts, towns, homes. Booze will also do it to college students.

Hard-line. Used by reporters or editors who don't like a guy's position or attitude. If they like him, he's committed, determined, solid, firm, steadfast or resolute.

Hardscrabble. "A wonderfully descriptive word," writes Mike Feinsilber of the AP, "but overdone." A proposal was made in the June 18, 2010, issue of *The Economist* to blacklist the word. "Today, it seems, anywhere and anything can be hardscrabble," *The Economist* noted. "A Google News search for the past month reveals a world teeming with hardscrabble lives, existences, times and circumstances; hardscrabble countries, land and soil; hardscrabble childhoods, upbringings, beginnings, roots and origins; a hardscrabble fishing community, hill town, burg, state, Indian reservation, various city neighbourhoods and an arrondissement of Paris (the 19th, if you must know)".

Head. When used by journalists, it means headline.

Heard around town. Hollywood and big city gossip columnist favorite. The writer may be the source, but he or she needs to lay blame elsewhere.

HEADLINESE

Columnar compression, the need to squeeze the heart of a story into a few words that attract readers' attention has created a subspecies of journalese known as headlinese. It's an art form that can create a kind of poetry. In his book *Alphabet Juice*, Roy Blount Jr. comments: "If literal newspapers die out, so will headlines like this one from *The Berkshire Eagle* of August 14,1998:

CANNIBALISM CASE
HAS SHRINK IN PICKLE

The story, by The Associated Press, began: "Illinois has moved to discipline a prominent psychiatrist accused of convincing a patient that she was a cannibal who ate human flesh meatloaf and who was the high priestess of a satanic cult."

Headlinese can also lead to confusion. As lexicographer Ben Zimmer wrote in *The New York Times,* January 10, 2010, "In their quest for concision, writers of newspaper headlines are inveterate sweepers away of little words, and the dust they kick up can lead to some amusing ambiguities. Legendary headlines from years past (some of which verge on the mythical) include 'Giant Waves Down Queen Mary's Funnel,' 'MacArthur Flies Back to Front' and 'Eighth Army Push Bottles Up Germans'."

Arnold Sawislak, a UPI Washington correspondent, gave headlinese full honor in his wonderful "novel of journalism," whose title was a headline a main character spent his career dreaming to use: *Dwarf Rapes Nun; Flees in UFO*. Published in 1985 (St. Martin's Press, New York), the novel remains, as its dust-cover says, "a rare and insightful glimpse into the riotous world of journalism."

Co-author Robert Skole's first job in journalism was reporting for the racy, irreverent Boston weekly, *The Mid-Town Journal*, famous for its double-entendre headlines of stories of the colorful adventures of city's uninhibited denizens. A story of a lady of the night winding up in the arms of the law after engaging in a jealousy-fueled boudoir tussle with two love-struck swains vying for her affections got this headline: "Three in Bed Tangle Lass".

With that, here are just a few favorite headlinese words, how they're used and what they really mean.

AXED. Cut, fired, reduced. Never used to describe what specifically occurred in an ax-murder.

BARBS. Politicians' favorite weapon to hurl at opponents. "Scott Brown's barbs draw Dems' fire," the *Boston Herald* told readers May 17, 2010.

BID. What a politician seeking office or a developer seeking permits do. Sometimes it's a buyer making an offer. Also, a city trying to get the Olympics, a political convention, or other major event.

BLAST. To criticize, condemn, rip or attack, especially when there's shouting and some profanity.

CHAIR. The electric chair: "Killer gets the chair". Also, popularly used instead of chairman or chairwoman, as "City Council seats new chair."

CHOP. To cut down or reduce, but rarely used to mean chop with an ax.

CONFAB. A meeting or conference.

CURB. To restrain, control, or rein in.

CURRY. When not the spice or dish, it's headlinese for boot-licking. Favor is always curried. Only editors who grew up on a ranch know what currying really means.

DECRY. Bellyaching or criticizing, when rip is too short, criticize too long and blast too tough.

DEMS Democrats as opposed to GOP.

DERAIL. Obligatory in a headline of a story about screw-ups of plans or projects of Amtrak or other railroads.

DUO. Two people, not necessarily musicians or singers. "Duo arrested after vandalizing McNabb's lawn" headlined a phillysportsforums.com story about two guys who evidently were not fans of Philadelphia Eagles quarterback Donovan McNabb.

EYE. To consider, ponder, look at or check out something.

FELLED. Got sick or died.

GAL. When not referring to a gallon of gas, it's a woman, used only in gossip or style pages.

GARNER. To collect or get something. Politicians always garner votes. "Flawed energy policy designed to garner votes," wrote *The Nation*, Apr. 20, 2011.

GIRD. Prepare; get ready. In the Bible it meant to put on armor and get set for battle.

GOP. Republicans, from the nickname "Grand Old Party."

GUY. A male, used mainly in light feature stories and style pages.

HAIL. Support, approve, cheer. Usually used when the paper likes what is hailed. Not to be confused with the frozen water the size of golf balls.

HAWK. To promote, push or lobby. Used when a lobbyist or group backs something the editor doesn't like. Something the editor likes is never hawked, but is advanced, aided, encouraged, helped, fostered or moved forward.

HEIST. A robbery or theft, but it must be a big one. "Police search for masked gunmen in jewelry heist," reported NBC from Los Angeles, Apr. 27, 2011.

HIKE. An increase in prices or taxes. Those who do the hiking are not called hikers.

HIT. When not on the sports or movie pages, or a story about a traffic accident, it means attack, usually political. "Mitt Romney gets hit by left and right on health care," reported *USA Today,* May 12, 2011.

HUB. Short for Boston, as "the Hub of the universe." Used almost exclusively by Boston writers. A Boston blog, universalhub.com, explains the origin: "First coined by writer Oliver Wendell Holmes, who actually referred to the State House as the hub of the solar system." Lost in Hub hubris is the fact that Holmes was being ironic. A classic apocryphal *Boston Globe* headline: "2 Hub men die in blast; New York also destroyed." And a real one in the *Boston Herald,* Mar. 22, 2011: "Farmers pitch catfish at Hub trade show."

HYPE. Promote, plug, publicize, or push something the paper doesn't like.

INK. To sign a contract. "Foes ink pact" is frequently used as an example of headlinese.

IRE. A popular word for anger, criticism. It's a bit tougher than irk, but just as short.

LULL. Favorite for quiet, suspended, pause. Old time United Press International reporters tell of the Stockholm office's getting a request from a newspaper client for a photo of General Lull, mentioned in a Vietnam report that a "general lull reigned" over a battle area. Stockholm relayed the request to New York, which could not locate a photo of the general, but asked their Washington and Saigon offices for help. Someone finally caught on. The newspaper copy editor who made the original request was a highly-admired practical joker.

MULL. Think about something.

NAB. What police do when they arrest someone.

NINE. A baseball team.

NIP. To stop, cut, shut off, usually done in the bud. When Tom Allen was with the *New York Daily News* he recalls someone in the composing room yelling, "Does anyone know a short word for 'hit?'"

NIX. Deny or reject. "Obama nixes Jesus" proclaimed foxnews.com, Dec. 22, 2009.

OUT. As a verb in headlines it means revealed, exposed, snitched on.

OUTAGE. Power failure.

PACT. Any contract, treaty or agreement.

PARLEY. To talk, discus, meet. "3000 Hindu leaders Parley at Allahabad," reported hinduismtoday.com.

PEN. To write, but rarely with a pen.

POLITICO. A politician, but never applied to one the editor admires.

POL. A politician the editor doesn't like.

POSE. A prediction something will happen, usually bad. "Parents on cellphones pose hazard," warned the South Florida *Sun-Sentinel* June 2, 2011.

PROBE. A verb or noun meaning investigation, usually by police. "Police probe fatal shooting at Finn McCool's," reported the *Scranton Times-Tribune*, May 17, 2011.

QUIZ. To ask more than one question.

RANKLE. Used when irk or roil is too short to fill a line. Also, when the stylebook says you can't write, "mad as hell." As *The Berkshire Eagle* headline put it Sept. 17, 2011: "Skaters rankle North Street merchants."

RAP. When not referring to a rapper's ryhmes, it's short for criticize or disparage. Also used as a noun for a criminal charge, such as a murder rap.

REVEL. Celebrate, usually with too much booze involved.

RIP. To criticize, condemn, attack.

ROUT. When not used in sports, it means somebody's armed forces got beat.

SCRUB. A plan, project or scheme got dumped.

SCUPPER. Nautical term, puzzling to landlubbers, meaning to ruin, screw up or otherwise send down the tubes. Handicapping an upcoming Iditarod, held when scuppers are iced solid, an *Anchorage Daily News* reporter may have been dreaming of summer when he wrote, "There is the simple factor of bad luck, which could easily scupper every musher's (including Mackey's) chances." The Mar. 1, 2009, story advised: "You can lay odds on a Mackey Iditarod win." (And Lance

Mackey, who won two previous races, was not scuppered, but did win that year's 1049-mile sled dog race, which invariably, outside Alaska, is described as "grueling". Alaskans don't need to be told it is.)

SEE. Forecasting something. "Politicians see damage to China relations," ABC News reported April 15, 2011.

SHRINK. When not referring to a psychiatrist, it means something got smaller or is fading. In sports, players' salaries may skyrocket, but a team's hopes often shrink.

SLAM. To criticize, condemn.

SLATED. Something planned. *The New York Times Manual of Style and Usage* by Allan M. Sigel and William Connolly advises: "Slate, as a verb meaning plan or schedule (The vote was slated for Thursday), is journalese and trite." Evidently, trite journalese won out, since a Times search for seven days in August, 2011, came up with over 10,000 references.

SLAY, SLAYER. Headlinese for kill, murder or killer, murderer.

SOAR. Stock prices soar unless they plunge or plummet.

SPAR. To debate, often by politicians.

SPUR. To push or prompt or start something, "Downpour spurs flooding in Haiti," AP reported in a photo cutline, Feb 17, 2011.

STIR. To get something started, usually trouble or opposition. Not politically correct to mean a jail.

STOKE. Something that intensifies something, such as fears, tension, anger, or opposition. Few readers under 60 realize that's what they do when they put more charcoal on the grill.

STUN. Useful word to mean anything from shock to astonishment to disbelief. Sports teams often stun an opponent.

SURGE. What the stock market does when it doesn't plummet.

SWOOP. What police do when they carry out a raid, despite language purists' insistence that only eagles can swoop.

TAP. To hire or select or draw money from a public treasury for a cause the paper doesn't like. When used as a noun it means buried or killed. "Taps for a bill to deduct veterinary costs." Reporters under 40 believe the word to with the gadgets the bartender pulls to draw a beer. Term has limited use outside of headlines: "Guess what honey, I was tapped for a promotion at work today!"

TIFF. Handy noun when spat has already been used for a fight that doesn't involve fists, knives or guns. "Obama-Brewer friction on display on tarmac tiff" reported *The Sacramento Bee*, Jan. 25, 2012. Lovers have tiffs, not brawls or battles, unless in court when they are ex-lovers. See also **Tarmac**.

TOIL. To work at a job the editor disapproves of, such as any job in a low-wage country.

TOT. A small child. Graeme Whitfield of the *Journal*, of Newcastle, UK, collects such examples and wrote in his newspaper on Mar. 1, 2008: "Type 'tot' into a Google News search, and you will get about six million hits. 'Choked tot bouncing back, dad says', says the *Honolulu Star*; 'Parents admit cruelty after tot swallowed drug', screams the *Reading Evening Post*. Yet I've never in my life heard anyone outside a newspaper office use the word 'tot'. 'My, what a nice tot you have there,' people never say. 'How old is your tot?'"

TOUT. A favorite verb when a group or promoter is pushing something that an editor doesn't 100 percent respect. Don't wait for one like this: "Pope touts peace in Yule rap." Mike Feinsilber of The Associated Press writes of tout: "It is a nice, short lead word. But to some (read that: me) it has a tawdry racetracky, carnivalish tone, maybe because it originally described the act of soliciting bets on a horserace. In any event, we tout too much. You'll never hear Aunt Hilda use 'tout.' From the AP wire: 'Obama has touted the tax credit as one of the big achievements of his first 100 days ... opening remarks in which he touted changes his fledgling administration already has made ... With pieces of wind turbine towers as a backdrop, Obama touted the small manufacturing firm.'"

TRAGEDY. Death.

TREMBLOR. An earthquake.

TROOPS. Armed forces in general, as "Troops mass on border". Can now also mean individual soldiers, a usage that irks old veterans, who would never say, "A troop was wounded" or "Two troops were honored..." The First Cavalry Division calls companies "troops" and cavalrymen "troopers". Boy and Girl Scouts still have troops, but the members of a troop are scouts.

UNREST. Anything from street demonstrations to rioting to civil war.

UP. Headlinese verb for increase.

VEX. Annoy, bother, bug.

VIE. To compete, contest, oppose, fight or battle.

WALL STREET. The financial industry.

WOE/WOES. Any trouble, problem or worry. "An excellent headline word because it's short," writes Frank Fellone of *The Arkansas Democrat-Gazette*. "A bad word to use in a sentence because it's, well, journalese."

WOO. A favorite past-time of politicians, whose romantic overtures are often declined. Businesses also try the tender approach. "Dentists Woo Runaway Patients With Foot Massage" reported the *Wall Street Journal*, Jan. 1, 2011. *The Boston Globe* racked up a headlinese five-bagger in one top story headline, Feb. 8, 2011: "Obama woos, exhorts, business. Urges firms to tap funds to add jobs; Mass groups hail vow of tax credits."

WRANGLE. A fight, squabble, argument. Unless they're from Texas, reporters don't know what a wrangler is.

Heart of Darkness. Metaphoric home of evil from the title of the Joseph Conrad novel. David Marsh writes in an article entitled, "Mind Your Language" in *The Guardian*, Feb. 14, 2010: "A colleague points out: 'It sometimes seems that any time anyone writes a piece about Africa (or, in fact, dark-skinned people), the first (and usually last) headline everyone comes up with is Heart of Darkness. It's unimaginative, and boring, but more importantly perpetuates lazy colonial attitudes, ideas of ignorance and benightedness, etc.'"

Heated exchange. A perfectly civilized discussion.

Heavy gunfire. This is the really dangerous stuff, unlike light gunfire which won't hurt anyone.

"He'll be missed." This anchor addendum to obits is favored by graduates of the "We're Crying Our Hearts Out for You" school of broadcasting, whose alumni proliferate on Los Angeles TV stations. The theory here is that "He'll be missed" is not insincere or deceptive because the deceased is bound to be missed by someone somewhere. Even though the anchor has never heard of this sucker and couldn't care less.

Helm. What a new boss or leader takes over, even if he or she doesn't know a helm from a keel. "New CEO takes the helm at biotech giant Amgen," reported *Bloomberg BusinessWeek*, May 23, 2012. However, some leaders are reported at the helm even though they were not at the helm when there was a helm available, as *The Arizona Daily Star* headlined, June 4, 2012, "Queen Elizabeth II at helm of colorful Jubilee flotilla."

Help us to understand. A PBS anchor's preferred way of asking, "Could you explain that in plain English?" As Judy Woodward, on May 6, 2011, asked a reporter, "Could you help us to understand the discrepancy?"

Hemorrhaging. Obligatory for losing money in any story about a hospital or health care. *The Berkshire Eagle,* Pittsfield, Mass., Feb 20, 2011, included the bleeding and cure in one lede: "With both hospitals and patients hemorrhaging increasing amounts of health care dollars, local and state officials say that Gov. Deval L. Patrick's new health-care-cost legislation might be the best medicine for the economy of the Commonwealth."

Hero. Just about anyone in uniform or someone who gets a cat down from a tree.

Hiccup. A screw-up. The hicupper is never identified. A major hiccup is a glitch.

High-powered. A big-shot who knows the Mayor.

High profile. Anyone or anything getting attention and is so well-known that the reporter feels obliged to mention it. As *The Baltimore Sun*, reported on Feb 8, 2012: "At the last home game before Baltimore's primary election in September, the mayor's guests included her chief political fundraiser, a high-profile lawyer whose firm donated generously to her campaign, and the head of a union who later appeared at a campaign event with her."

High rate of speed. Fast.

High tech. Originally, anything that contained a transistor and silicon. Now applied to everything from coffee makers to toilet brushes.

High-speed chase. All police chases are at high speeds. It would be big news, such as the O.J. Simpson chase, if a chase stayed within speed limits.

Highly regarded. One degree below highly respected. His mother boasts about him.

Highly respected. One degree above highly regarded. His mother and father both boast about him.

Hikes. Tax increases, an example noted by the late William Safire on several occasions.

Hint. Reporter speculates that something might bring on something else, which is often obvious. "Campaign finance reports give hint into Republicans' presidential hopefuls and their

viability," was the *Chicago Tribune's* insightful headline over an AP story, July 15, 2011.

Hired guns. Lobbyists, lawyers or flacks for a cause or company the reporter doesn't like. Otherwise, they are advocates, supporters or spokesmen. "Here's what Ocean Spray's hired guns have to say," reported huffingtonpost.com, June 5, 2012, in a story about sugar content of cranberry juice.

Historic. All treaties, agreements and international meetings between heads of state, most of which will be forgotten in a few months, except by the reporter who will frequently remind guys at the press club bar that he covered the historic event. Also used when the reporter can't think of a similar occurrence. Ten readers will email to say the thing happened a dozen times in the past. Often used to describe a place or event that everyone knows is historic, as Dennis Byrne, Chicago writer, reminded readers of the chicagonow.com blog, May 31, 2011, that Harry Truman "made the historic decision to use nuclear weapons against Japan."

Hit man. Political correct police insist this is a sexist term, and descriptions as "hired gun" or "hired killer" should be used instead. But women got their share of the action in a *Philadelphia Inquirer* story, Sept 10, 2011, headlined "New Jersey woman admits hiring hit man with stolen credit cards."

Hit the market. What something does when it is released for sale or is first put on TV or in the press. A web search of "hit the market" got three million citations, including this one: "Entire Italian village hits the market for less than $1M."

Holds sway. To rule. It sounds benign, but quite often its sway held by guns, murder and terror. Writing about the arrest of Mexican killer Jose de Jesus Mendez Vargas, "widely known as El Chango, or The Monkey," *The San Antonio News Times*, on June 22, 2011, commented, "Mendez's arrest hardly means immediate peace in the territories where La Familia holds sway." Where a reporter is sympathetic with a dictator, ruler or ruling party, they "hold sway." Those dictatorships or tyrannies not approved of "rule with an iron hand."

Hone. Skills and talents are supposedly being improved. Few living reporters have ever honed a razor.

Hopeless. A situation the reporter doesn't like. In a Jan 24, 2012, *Des Moines Register* commentary, headlined, "Iowa, fields of hopeless dopers," columnist Mike Draper, explained, "I mean, to say Iowa is a hopeless dump filled with meth addicts and wasteoids is like calling New Jersey tolerable... The other night, I met with the University of Iowa's School of Journalism over Jello-O and crank. They were worried that their new parody and satire major was off to a rough start. "We need you, Mike," they said. "Will you teach in Iowa City?" "Stay in Iowa?" I asked. "Good God no."

Hot-button. Any subject in which there is controversy.

"How does it feel?" Standard question by a reporter who can't think of an intelligent question. Usually asked to a sports champion, to someone named a Nobel Prize winner or to a person achieving a historic record, as "How does it feel to be the first human to catch a

Frisbee thrown from the top of the Eiffel Tower?" Contributor Stanley Bloom, a former Stockholm radio reporter, writes: "A soccer manager once complained to me about the question being put to him again and again by different journalists after his team had won the Swedish championship. 'How do they think I bloody-well feel?' he said. The manager was an Englishman."

"How do you reply to those who say_____?" Reporter doesn't have the guts to ask a tough question, so he or she puts it in an anonymous mouth.

Howl. What winds, wolves and coyotes do. Politicians often do the same, but are never described as howling.

Huddle. How folk living in small towns in the far north survive the long, cold winter months. People living in the Sunbelt never huddle.

Huge. In the sporting press, something that used to be big or great. Sometimes now expressed as the compound modifier huge-huge. "Once upon a time a basket made as the shot clock expired was huge. Now it may be huge-huge," deputy editor Frank Fellone of *The Arkansas Democrat-Gazette* has said, then asks, "What can be more huge than huge-huge? Oh, the drama of language abuse."

Hulking. Anything large requiring an effort by the reporter to find the exact dimensions or an accurate description. A "hulking tanker" is easier than reporting the tanker's length, beam and deadweight tonnage. All parking garages are hulking. A monstrous building by an architect or developer the reporter likes is never hulking.

Human error. Error not made by an animal or a machine. The human who screwed up is usually anonymous, unless the person at the top can find someone to take the blame.

Humanitarian aid. Supplies sent to a warring party whom the reporter sympathizes with. The other side gets plain old-fashioned aid or worse, "assistance that can be used by the military."

Humorous. Critics' description of a film with a few light moments. Promoted as "the comedy of the year."

Hunker down. What folks do when a storm approaches.

Hurl. How demonstrators throw rocks, paving blocks or cobblestones.

Hush. What concert halls are before the orchestra starts playing. Libraries, churches, historic homes are always hush. Hush money is just as quiet, as long as it's kept hush hush.

Hustings. Word which is trotted out every time a major electoral campaign gets underway. It is an archaic way of saying that someone is out making speeches in the boondocks.

Hurdles. Something in the way; usually the other political party or a public agency. People face hurdles even though they are sitting at a desk trying to figure out ways to avoid jumping someplace.

Icon. See *iconic*. Icon is one of the terms singled out in the *Reuters Handbook of Journalism* as journalese to be avoided.

Iconic. Hyperbolic adjective for famous or well-known. It is so overused that there will soon be no public building or celebrity who will not be celebrated as iconic. Frank Fellone, deputy editor of *The Arkansas Democrat-Gazette,* wrote in the Mar. 1, 2011, edition of his newspaper: "About 20 years ago, this adjective, and the equally lame noun, crept into and overcame news writing. In this newspaper, as an example, we have recently described as iconic a segment of the Little Rock marathon, the shape of a lamp, an expressionistic painting, a baseball player, a recipe that includes chocolate, a bridge that hasn't been built or even designed, a brewery whose best-selling product is a light swill, an actor, a bison herd and the chain smokers of France."

This is AP's Mike Feinsilber's take that he titled, *Ironic, Iconic and Other Words we Love Too Much:* "What word describes: Bart Simpson, Oregon's Mount Hood, General Motors, an unnamed slave ship at the Smithsonian, Newt Gingrich, Merrill Lynch & Co., the wild horses of the American West, Michelle Obama, failed banks and Marion Barry? On the AP wire, under Washington datelines in recent weeks, all have been called 'icons.' Or 'iconic.' Time for an iconoclast on the desk."

Illegal. As a noun, any non-citizen an editor thinks should be deported. This does not apply to the editor's gardener, house-cleaner, or cook at a favorite ethnic eatery.

Ill-fated. Anything that has crashed and whose wreckage is now being sifted through by federal investigators.

Illusions. The paper doesn't approve of a proposal by politicians or developers. Illusions are always shattered. See also *Grand illusions*.

Image grab. Jargon for taking a still photo from a video.

Imaginative. Film critics' favorite for a confusing story.

Immeasurable. Reporter believes something is either so small or so large it can't be measured. Risks reported as immeasurably small will prompt a dozen emails to the editor saying the risks are large and can be measured.

Impaired. Politically correct for drunk, drugged or disabled.

Important. Anything a reporter wants the public to think it was worth the time to report, even though it wasn't. As "In an important speech today, the mayor said the city would hire three additional parking meter officers."

Imposing. A large person or structure, when the reporter is impressed. Otherwise, it's *hulking*.

Impromptu. Disorganized, confused or ill-advised. "In an impromptu airport press conference, the Congressman defended his two week, mid-winter, fact-finding trip to Bermuda as essential to national security."

Improvement. Any plan or project the paper likes.

In a or **On a**. The NPR classic start of a story, setting the scene first and getting to the real facts or news much later. "In a poverty-stricken village in the remote Andes, a toothless peasant..." This style has been widely adopted by print feature writers.

In depth. A long; wordy story, such as one revealing that a politician is a liar and a crook, which everyone knew all along, The paper submits such stories for a Pulitzer. In TV news, the term applies to any story lasting more than 90 seconds.

In harm's way. Where a volunteer puts himself when joining the military or a police or fire department. Kids in harm's way are usually rescued by quick-thinking heroes.

In recent memory. Everyone else has gone home, the library is locked, Google gives me zilch, and this is the only thing the reporter can think of that hasn't happened before. The paper will get a dozen emails saying the same thing happened five years ago.

In the shadow of. Where the children or spouses of the rich and famous stand. For example, Frank Sinatra Jr. or Ted Kennedy Jr. Applies also to poverty that exists within any measurable distance of the White House or other government buildings, the existence of which the people inside these buildings are totally indifferent.

In the streets. Where action takes place in riots, demonstrations or civil wars. Often used for large display headlines over photos from overseas. "Chaos in the streets," "Anger in the streets," "Heartbreak in the streets." See *The street*.

In what could be. Reporter as a forecaster with a bit of a hedge, as the *Tampa Bay Times* reported June 9, 2012, "In what could be the most watched race in the county, five candidates qualified to run for Hillsborough County appraiser."

Inappropriate relationship. A politician or top executive is having sex with someone on the staff who is not his or her spouse.

Incentive. Extra money that gets something going, such as a subsidy or pay-off.

Inch up. Any kind of increase even if it's not measured in inches or feet. Gas prices always inch up, never inch down.

Incident. Anything on a police report, from a barking dog complaint to a murder.

Incredible. TV reporters' favorite to describe stories about a survival or journey or discovery. Of course, if it's incredible, should you believe it?

Indefatigable. A real pest; someone who calls the reporter at home during the World Series to complain about something the town council did a week earlier.

Inevitable. This is what the newspaper has been saying for six months.

Influential. A group or association that is so influential that the reporter feels obliged to tell the reader it is.

Innocence was lost. What happens when an historic event shocks a people or nation, such as an assassination, attack or riot. Innocence can be lost any number of times. See *Lost innocence*.

Innovation. Anything new.

Inside the Beltway. Term used by Washington correspondents to refer to themselves and the people they lunch with. Outside the Beltway refers to the rest of the country. The Beltway, the circular highway ringing Washington, is best known by locals for trailer trucks overturning and snarled traffic.

Insisted. Yeah, yeah, wink, wink, nudge, nudge. Wrongly claimed. Or, as reporter Joseph Goulden explains: "*Insisted* is a signal word by which a reporter tells readers: 'This is what the guy says, but we of superior wisdom do not believe him.'" He gives an example of a Florida newspaper story that said, "At that time, Scott had insisted that overruns could end up costing his state more than $3 billion."

Interact. Talk to someone. Or give him the finger. Or punch him in the nose.

Interactive. You can play a game with the gadget, which usually beats you.

Interestingly. Dig this point. The rest of the article is of no interest and will put you to sleep.

Intimate relationship. They're having sex.

Intricate. Complicated material beyond the comprehension of the reporter, who couldn't find someone to explain it in simple English. Joseph Goulden says that in his *Philadelphia Inquirer* days it would be reported as, "Documents indicating financial dealings of an intricate nature were entered into evidence."

Involved. If involved with someone whom a guy or girl should not be involved with, it means a love affair.

Irascible. Big-mouth smart-ass.

Irksome. A royal pain in the neck, often reinforced as "most irksome."

Iron fist. What dictators rule with, sometimes, but not often, in a velvet glove.

Ironically. Oddly, strangely, coincidentally. Rarely used according to its main dictionary definition: conveying the opposite of its literal meaning.

Irreverent. Swears and shouts a lot.

Issue. Just about anything can be an issue. Useful when a short word is needed in a headline. Often used by public relations people, and repeated by reporters, to describe a major calamity, trouble or catastrophe, such as, "Toyota's acceleration issue."

Is thought to be. Reporter got bored with "is believed to be" or "many say..."

It is tempting to speculate. A favorite of writers of scientific papers. Martin Dworkin, Professor Emeritus, Department of Microbiology, University of Minnesota, points out that this is never followed by, "But I have resisted the temptation."

Jaw-dropping. Reporter says you're going to be so shocked you'll look like an idiot with your mouth wide open. "In a jaw-dropping announcement, the Mayor said he'll hire his brother-in-law as his driver."

Jihad. Any campaign against something. "Menino's Wal-Mart jihad" was the headline of a *Boston Herald* column: about the mayor, who, in the old days, would be "on the war path" against the retail firm. War path, of course, is no longer politically correct. The *AP Stylebook* definition of jihad: "Arabic noun used to refer to the Islamic concept of the struggle to do good. In particular situations, that can include holy war, the meaning extremist Muslims commonly use."

Jockeying. What politicians do when they're busy elbowing out an opponent. No politician outside of Texas or Kentucky is known to have ever been a jockey.

Journo. Journalist slang for journalist. One old definition of a journalist is, "A reporter looking for work." Simply "J" is a nickname for a student at the University of Missouri School of Journalism. Stephanie Callahan, a former J, says, "A J can be identified by his or her pea coat, skinny jeans, horn-rimmed glasses, over-the-shoulder satchel, and an attitude toward anyone who doesn't have an opinion."

Jump-start. A project finally gets going, often with politicians taking credit. Most people under 30 have no idea how to jump-start a car with a dead battery.

Jump through hoops. Complicated. What bureaucrats or giant companies make people do to get something corrected.

Junket. Trips paid for by someone else, taken by politicians the reporter doesn't like. If the reporter is a politician's pal, it's a trade mission or an exhaustive study tour. Journalists never accept junkets. They go on press tours.

Junky. Anyone addicted to or deeply interested in something, such as a political junky or a news junky or sports junky. It is not politically correct to call a drug addict a junky—the original junky. Dope fiend is definitely out.

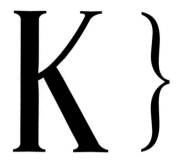

Key. Anything the reporter thinks is important, such as key ally, key economic indicator, key cleaning lady for the mayor's office.

Knock down. How firefighters put out a fire.

Known as / or. Any new technology, drug, treatment, chemical compound or organization with a long name is always given its own identifying letters, such as "The technology, known as Rapid Thermal Processing, or RTP..." in *The Berkshire Eagle*, Pittsfield, Mass., and "Massachusetts Marketing Partnership, or MMP..." the *Boston Herald*, both Feb 25, 2011. Explosives contain hexamethylene triperoxide diamine or HMTD and triacetone triperoxide or TATP.

Known for. A reporter's way of labeling someone or something without giving a source. It's usually something every reader or viewer already knows, such as, "The Senator, who is known for putting his relatives on the city payroll, ..."

Kumbaya. A newer version of Hallelujah!

{L

Labor of love. The province of lost causes and borderline crazies. A Gale Powersearch of newspapers shows 3,469 such labors dating back to 1985. Often applied to troublesome shopping decisions for wedding anniversaries and Valentine's Day.

Labyrinthine. Complex and complicated, as all legislation is. "Steve Zito knew it was a huge undertaking," reported the *Commercial Appeal* of Memphis, Dec 7, 2009. "The mere idea of helping to push a bill through the labyrinthine halls of the state legislature was, to his knowledge, unprecedented in his business."

Lambast: To criticize. In his blog *Journalese-English Dictionary,* Graeme Whitfield used this example from BBC online: "Ferguson right to lambast football agents or are they simply doing their job?" He added that it would never be said in real life: "I lambast you for that terrible decision."

Landmark. A reporter wants it known he or she is covering big stuff, such as a piece of legislation, a school board decision, or a business deal. A landmark is rarely just a landmark.

Land of contrasts. Said of all foreign countries by travel writers.

Most of these countries also feature "a blend of the old and the new."

Landscape. What a politician works in.

Large numbers of. Reporter has no idea whatsoever the number of people, dogs, coyotes, birds or whatever he or she is writing about, but there are more than two.

Larger than life. A big mouth publicity-hound with a lot of money.

Larger truth. The exclusive preserve of journalists who invoke this concept after a few facts have been mangled. Writing of this in a 1984 *Time* essay, Roger Rosenblatt said, "When journalists hear journalists claim a 'larger truth', they really ought to go for their pistols." Alistair Reid wrote a classic definition in *The New Yorker*: "A reporter might take liberties with the factual circumstances to make the larger truth clear."

Laundry list. A long rap sheet, table of budget appropriations, or other inventory. Readers under 40 have never seen a real laundry list. As noted by Philip Corbett, who is in charge of *The New York Times*' style manual, the term doesn't simply mean a long list. "It suggests a list that's random or unselective (like your pile of dirty clothes)," he says. "But don't substitute 'litany,' which has become a cliché itself and refers to a repetitive recitation, as a prayer's series of petitions. If you are writing about a long list, how about describing it as 'a long list'?"

Lede. JOURNOSPEAK for "lead", the opening sentence of a story. It is pronounced lead, to rhyme with feed.

Legend has it. The press doesn't deal with legends unless they

LIFESTYLE PARTIES

DEEP TRANSLATION for Charity Events, which used to be known as Society Parties. Elaine Viets, mystery novelist, formerly of *The St. Louis Post-Dispatch*, offers these insights.

A STUNNING GOWN: Low-cut. Also, too tight.

BUBBLY: Brainless, flighty.

COLORFUL: A gentleman who appears in ads for his own business; one who wears gold brocade dinner jackets.

COZY: 400 of the 500 people invited did not show up.

DANCED TILL DAWN: The press went home early.

DANCED TO THE BIG BAND SOUND OF ... Not a musician under 60.

ELEGANT: Ordinary. The usual crowd. Also, boring.

FAMILY AFFAIR: The guest list is positively incestuous.

FAMILY AFFAIR, CATHOLIC: The bishop is present.

FESTIVE: Drunk

FLAMBOYANT: Overdressed. Also, drunk.

GRACIOUS: Panting to have her name in the paper.

HONORARY CHAIR: Does no work. The committee hopes his or her name will sell tickets.

INFORMAL: Disorganized. Also, homemade.

INTIMATE: Couldn't sell tickets.

LAVISH: The charity gets zilch.

LEISURELY: Tedious.

LIVELY: Drunk.

MAJESTIC: Fat.

ORIGINAL: When used to describe food, it means "I've never seen anything like this before. Not on a table anyway."

QUEENLY: Fat.

REGAL: Stuck up.

SIMPLE: Cheap.

SPORTY: Nothing he's wearing matches.

STATUESQUE: Fat.

STILL YOUTHFUL: Looks terribly old. Not to be confused with a youthful companion. That means cradle-robbing.

STRIKING: Can't believe anyone would dress like that.

TASTEFUL: Stuffy. Monogrammed.

VIVACIOUS: Drunk.

WE'RE HAVING A WONDERFUL TIME: Used to indicate acute ennui.

---

concern "legendary" things like drinking or hanky panky.

Legendary. An individual who did something so long ago that the reporter had to go to Google to find out what it was.

Less forthcoming. Not willing to comment; tight lipped.

Leverage. Influence. Money.

Life savings. "Any sum in excess of about $50 taken by thieves from a poor person is automatically described in the press as 'life savings'," According to Fritz Spiegel, in *Keep Taking the Tabloids: What the papers say and how they say it*.

Likely. Reporter as a fortune teller, too lazy to get direct quotes. As an AP story reported from Tokyo about Princess Aiko's being bullied by schoolmates: "The story is likely to shock the Japanese."

Likelihood. The crystal ball again. "Adding menthol to cigarettes may increase the likelihood of addiction and make it easier for young people to start smoking," reported the *Chicago Tribune*, Mar. 2, 2011.

Lincolnesque. Any politician, at least six feet tall, with a good head of hair and a horse face. It doesn't matter what he says as long as he has a deep voice and speaks slowly.

Line in the sand. A definite limit established by a politician or leader. Usually, the line will shift along with the sand.

Linked. Not quite alleged, but close to it. "Feds indict 5 linked to Miami escort business", headlined *The Miami Herald*, July 22, 2010.

Literally. Journalese for something that actually or truly occurred. One might assume that anything else in the story not specifically identified as literally is doubtful at best and false at worst. But do not take everything literally that is identified as literally. The July 19, 2011, *The Boston Globe* arts section cover story was a two-page shocker, headlined: "Please make it stop. Literally. Misuse of the word has spread to Stanley Cup celebrations and even a sitcom character." Reporter Christopher Muther warned: "There is a good chance the incorrect use of the word eventually will eclipse its original definition." Horrors! But why has this catastrophe taken so long? Muther traces the misuse to the 18th and 19th centuries, and he provides an 1839 example from none other than Charles Dickens.

In the article, Ben Zimmer, executive producer of the Visual Thesaurus and vocabulary.com,

commented: "I go on a lot of talk shows, and people complain about the usual suspects. It's 'literally' and 'hopefully' that people complain about. But there are many other words that are commonly used: 'truly,' 'positively,' 'absolutely.' But those words don't stick in people's craw the way that 'literally' does." Zimmer used as examples two Boston Bruins hockey players who incorrectly used "literally" in their exuberance over winning the Stanley Cup. This could qualify Zimmer as the team's unofficial language coach. A Google search of "*Christopher Muther*" and "*literally*" got 1,200 hits. A sampling of his usages showed he literally knows his stuff: all that the *Journalese* authors checked were correct, but we are not sure about the 3.3 million hits for "*The Boston Globe*" and "*literally.*"

Little girl or **Little boy**. Young kids are not simply girls or boys. They are always, "The 2-year-old little girl...." or "A 3-year-old little boy...."

Little-known. Used when a reporter is showing off and saying here is something I know, but you don't. *CBS-TV* news on Feb 15, 2012, called the SWIFT international financial transfer system "little-known", and then went on to report that it is used millions of times a day worldwide.

Little-publicized. Just discovered, no thanks to the subject of the story who is too cheap to hire a PR agency.

Live ammunition. Bullets or shells. Also called live rounds. What a tyrant's police or military respond with when there's a demonstration or riot. If they fired blanks, it would be real news.

Local man or **Local woman**. Good for headlines and ledes when "local" is anywhere in a huge metropolitan area, or to avoid repeating the city name. Locals always seems to be dying or getting killed or in the news someplace else. "Local man remembers time as pilot for Bin Laden family," reported *KABB Fox 26 News*, San Antonio, May 16, 2011.

Lock horns. Politicians in a debate in which they inevitably trade barbs. Although "lock horns" originated from elk or deer proving machismo, when politicians do so, it would more appropriately project an image of bulls.

Logjam. Term used exclusively with litigation (courtroom logjam) and lawmaking (legislative logjam). The last time it was used to describe a pile-up of logs in a river was when Harry Truman was in the White House.

Long-awaited. There's been a lot of foot-dragging since the news outlet told you about this. It is not clear who has done the waiting, but it is more likely the reporter than the reader.

Longtime. A title given to an "observer" or "consultant" who is always available, usually not identified, and whose comments are predictable, inaccurate or pure hot air. Observers are often the reporter's alter-ego. Charlie Cook of the *National Journal* reported, Oct. 9, 2010: "More than a few longtime observers who saw 1994 up close and personal are watching now. They will tell you...."

Loom. Something horrible may happen. But no headline writer will ever bet that it will happen.

Lord. Usually a drug boss or slum owner.

Lost innocence. Unlike a human, a nation can lose its innocence more than once. A Swedish newspaper counted the times that peaceful Sweden, according to news reports, "lost its innocence": after a Yugoslavian ambassador was murdered in Stockholm in the early 1980s; after a hi-jacking of a Swedish airplane resulted in freeing the killers; after the German Embassy in Stockholm was taken over by Red Army Faction terrorists a few years later; after Prime Minister Olof Palme was murdered in 1986; after Foreign Minister Anna Lind was murdered in 2003; and in December, 2010, when an Islamic suicide bomber tried to kill large numbers of Swedes in downtown Stockholm. Those were just a few times Sweden's innocence was lost.

Low-cut dress. Every lifestyle story of a charity event contains details about what the women wore, but not the men, unless the guy made an ass of himself by wearing an orange necktie to a St. Patrick's Day reception for the Prime Minister of Ireland at the White House.

Low-hanging fruit. Easy pickings. Politicians always reach for this first.

Lush. Lots of grass, trees, swamp or jungle, as "lush green wetlands". Never used for a drunk except in a direct quote.

Luxury. Obligatory description of any new condo, co-op or rental apartment. If designated "affordable" it means the developer got public funds to finance the project, which will be affordable only to those with enough money.

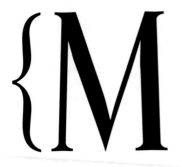

Machiavellian. Any action by politicians the paper does not support. Politicians the paper does support are wise, savvy, strategic, shrewd or astute players of the political game.

Magic bullet. Panacea, cure-all—but invariably stated in the negative. *Magic bullet* is one of the terms singled out as avoidable journalese in the *Reuters Handbook of Journalism*.

Magnate. A person with a big business. He'll be elevated to a *baron* elsewhere in the story. "Auto magnate sells Back Bay brownstone for 8.75M," the *Boston Herald* headlined, Feb 13, 2011, and the story begins: "Car baron Herb Chambers..."

Main street. The local economy as contrasted with Wall Street

Mainstream media. The major papers and TV networks and websites, which, according to critics, are biased and never publish or broadcast news and feature stories that the critics say should be printed and broadcast, although the critics boast they never read or view the mainstream media newspapers or TV news or websites. Also abbreviated, MSM.

Maintain. The subject said it and the reporter would add "wink, wink, nudge, nudge" if he or she could get away with it. See also *Insisted*.

Major study. Term used for all studies that get reported, even minor ones and just plain old-fashioned studies. Just about everything that shows up on the pages of *The New England Journal of Medicine* is called a "major study". Such studies are likely to contradict the findings of the previous "major study" on the subject. (Quick! What did the last major study say on the health effects of coffee?)

Make sense of. What reporters say people are trying to do after something completely senseless and horrific happens.

Makes you wonder. TV anchors' obligatory comment after a story about someone doing something goofy.

Manifestly. Something that's obvious, and the reporter figures he or she must tell you that it's obvious, which you wouldn't know until he or she points it out.

Many. If a reporter has absolutely no idea exactly how many, it's simply "many", as in "Many in Washington say...." or "Many New Yorkers believe..." If the reporter doesn't like what "many" are saying, it will be "Few say..." Such loaded, subjective, vague, generalizations were once banned by tough copy editors who would toss the story back to the reporter and demand, "How many?" Those editors no longer exist. A search of *The New York Times* articles for the 12 months ending May 25, 2011, got 8,850 hits for "Many say" and over 10,000 for "Many New Yorkers" and "Many believe" but only 2,040 for "Many think," which indicates that *Times* reporters feel there are relatively few who think. Our search did not break down how many were direct quotes or in op-ed pieces or letters. That can be a journalism school professor's assignment to the next Reporting 101 student who writes "Many say..." However the student might refer the professor to the *Columbia Journalism Review*. A quick search of its excellent search facility turned up 218 hits for "many reporters" in *CJR* articles and 32 hits for "many editors." *Columbia Journalism Review* is published by the Columbia University Graduate School of Journalism. See also **Some say**.

Marathon. Coupled with round-the-clock, this is the kind of bargaining session that weary negotiators conduct before often reaching eleventh-hour agreements that narrowly avert a strike. No negotiations have ever been held while running those 26.2 miles. This metaphor was singled out in the *Reuters Handbook of Journalism* as journalese to be avoided. Since the marathon was first run in Greece, its use could be appropriate in this Athens datelined AP story, as reported by cbsnews.com, Feb 9, 2012: "A spokeswoman for Papademos' office said the deal will allow alternatives to the pension cuts rejected early Thursday during a marathon meeting of coalition party leaders."

Marching orders. The CEO, mayor or governor told layabouts to get off their butts and start working. Used by reporters who were never in the military and have no idea what marching orders are.

Market solutions. Capitalism at its best or worst, depending on the reporter's view. Fancy term is "laissez faire."

Marred. When a politician gets 10 years in jail for fraud, his or her career is marred. Also, something the reporter doesn't like, as "the area marred by concrete highway ramps."

Marshall Plan. This program to help rebuild Western Europe after World War II still stands as one of the most over-used clichés by editorial writers. "What we need is a *Marshall Plan* to..." Also, "If we can send a man to the moon..."

Massacre. "Any firing of two or more political types on the same day" was the definition given by John Leo in an essay on "Reporterspeak" in *U.S. News & World Report* in 1968. In sports, a routing. Also, mass murder.

Master thieves. Crooks who don't get caught until they are caught.

Masterful. Book reviewer favorite when riveting, gripping, compelling have been used.

Maw. What money, usually public, is poured into when the writer doesn't like it. When he or she approves the recipient, the money is invested.

May. Reporter predicts something that might possibly happen, such as "may raise questions," or "may renew speculation" or "may draw criticism." Follow-up stories say, "As expected..." If it doesn't happen, there is no follow-up story.

Mecca. Any place worshipped by anybody, such as "an ice cream lover's mecca" or "a surfboarder's mecca." It sometimes refers to the Islamic holy city—the actual Mecca.

Meddling. Congress or a state legislature or city council doing something the paper doesn't like. If the paper approves of it, it becomes a long-overdue regulatory action.

Media circus. Event that, to the consternation of beat reporters, has drawn more than one television camera. For television people, a media circus is any event that attracts the traditional networks, the cable news channels and a few print reporters. A real media circus features an open bar and free buffet.

Media representative. A reporter. Distinction between a media representative and a reporter is that the media representative never spills a drink while a reporter never refuses one.

Mentioned. Common term used to describe a politician who is planning to run for office. If you read that a person has been "mentioned" as a possible Senate candidate, this means that the reporter has already gotten eight phone calls, 12 press releases and two personal visits from the eager office-seeker.

Mentor. At least one mentor must be mentioned in all articles about successful women in business. The woman must also be able to "network" and "dress for success."

Mercurial. Wild. Usually applied to a looney dictator. "The mercurial Saleh, who ruled Yemen for more than three decades...," wrote foxnews.com, Jan. 22, 2012. But athletes can also win that adjective. *USA Today,* in an AP story about Vernon Davis, reported that same day: "The 49ers' mercurial tight end scored the first touchdown in Sunday's NFC Championship Game in the first quarter."

Message. Three or four commercials, as, "We now pause for this message."

Metaphor. A reporter showing off that he or she once stayed awake in a course on creative writing. "Seattle's 'Machine' a metaphor in motion for Burning Man fest," headlined *The Seattle Times*, Aug. 6, 2005.

Meteorologist. The weatherman or weatherwoman. One who makes a living by honing a fine distinction between "partly sunny" and "partly cloudy".

Metrics. Numbers. Statistics. Data. In an analysis of "Advanced metrics in sports," Matt Hursh in blogtensports.com offered this truth that will screw up the most beautiful mathematics: "But one misstep or dropped ball by their opponents could make them look great instead of terrible. This is why you can't always trust the numbers when it comes to football." Business writers have also discovered metrics. "Stocks are soaring, but investors who buy in now may still be getting a deal of a decade, based on metrics of how pricey the market is," according to Matt Krantz, in *USA Today*, Feb.9, 2012. Journalists who use the term "metrics" might be puzzled at the Merriam-Webster dictionary definition of the word: "A part of prosody dealing with metrical structure."

Mighty. Any river with a hydro power plant. Said also of rivers with old paper or textile mills alongside them. The Mississippi is always mighty.

Middle names. Only assassins seem to have them.

Mid-life crisis. Any guy over 40 who loses his head over a hot babe. The affliction, undoubtedly under study by geneticists, is commonly suffered by politicians and preachers.

Mild-mannered. Deeply introverted; mousey. The kiss of death if a football coach is described this way.

Milestone. Anything the reporter thinks is an important development, such as milestone legislation requiring dog owners to clean up poop. In some cases, it's good that real milestones no longer exist, as illustrated by this *Wall Street Journal* headline, June 9, 2012, "Boeing Hits a Milestone."

Militant. Heavily-armed individual that the paper likes. If the guy is militant in the paper's own country, he's a terrorist. See also *Activist, Fighter* and *Holds sway*.

Military precision. Thieves, who are professionals, pull off heists this way, but often forget that in every parade there's always one marcher out of step.

Minder. A cop or official assigned to control a foreign reporter in a dictatorship.

Mine. To dig, but not necessarily for coal or minerals. "Making it easier for publishers to mine the popular mobile services for more revenue," reported the AP, Feb 16, 2011, on Apple apps.

Mishap. Something terrible with long-lasting consequences. Three Mile Island, Chernobyl and Fukushima were widely described as "nuclear station mishaps". In the past, such events would have been called disasters. Meanwhile, disaster is applied to plays or movies that flop or baseball teams that lose three games in a row.

Misidentified. "Boy, did we screw up!" Corrections editor explains that the photo of the governor's wife was not that of a linebacker signed by the Colts.

Misquoted. A politician's favorite claim, which reporters and editors scoff at, even though they forgot to switch on their tape recorders that would have proven the politician was right.

Misstated. Correction column euphemism for "We reported it so cockeyed we're forced to admit it."

Mob boss. Always reputed, which sounds good, even though the mug would never win a libel suit because he has a record a mile long. A mob boss is any gangster the FBI says is a mob boss. All mob bosses have nicknames, given in quotation marks to enhance the story, such as "Scarface", "Greasy Thumb", "The Cheeseman", "The Rifleman", "Baby Shanks". If the mobster has no such nickname, the FBI will make up one for media use. Cops' or prosecutors' nicknames are never reported, even if everyone uses them.

Modest. Term applied to most houses and salaries. It has been observed that journalese decrees all houses are either modest or stately.

Momentum. An athlete, team or political candidate making progress, but momentum tends to get mentioned only when it is being lost. Known as "Big Mo."

Monetize. To make money. "Stipple Marketplace enables publishers to monetize any image on their website," media blog Poynter.org reported Sept. 20, 2011.

Monitor. Reporters' favorite for officials' promises to keep an eye on something. They actually will do less monitoring than a hall monitor in a middle school. Also used by TV newscasters to mean they'll continue to cover a developing story.

Moral outrage. A quality of outrage reserved for editors of rarely-read publications with which, nevertheless, the writer is in complete agreement.

More than. The reporter doesn't know the exact number, other than a minimum estimate, and his or her editor doesn't care. "The phrase is useful in many contexts but is sometimes opinionated," writes *The New York Times Manual of Style and Usage*: "More than is also imprecise.

More than $100,000 can mean $101,000 or $500,000. Specifics are preferred." However, *The AP Sylebook*, in discussing the word *over* ("generally refers to spatial relationships, *The plane flew over the city*) advises: "*More than* is preferred with numerals. *Their salaries went up more than $20 a week.*" Ignoring the *Times* and AP stylebooks, *The Boston Globe* ran a cutline, Sept 1, 2011: "Over 3,400 new citizens from more than 130 countries took the oath of allegiance..."

Mother nature. Meteorologists' favorite for weather when they can't forecast it or when she is out of control. "Carroll County and Frederick County residents are among those picking up the pieces after Mother Nature's weekend rampage," reported *WBAL* Baltimore, Apr 18, 2011.

Motion picture. A very serious film the reviewer likes, and is often described as a "major motion picture." Otherwise, it's a movie or film or flick.

Mounting. What things do when they increase. John Leo wrote in 1968 that this verb is always followed by one of three words— "concern, pressure or deficits." See also *Numbers*.

Move forward. A politician's favorite dodge, which reporters never follow up with, "Exactly what do you mean by move forward?" Nothing ever moves backward.

Movers and shakers. Big shots, well-connected to politicians and to each other, even if what they move and shake is rather limited, as the *Sacramento Bee* reported, June 8, 2012, "The SacTown Dining Collective formed with the idea of mobilizing local food movers and sharers to show how much culinary talent exists in this town."

Much-maligned. Seldom simply maligned, often applied to lesser vegetables in newspaper food sections. Example: A *Washington Post,* May, 1986, food feature on the "much-maligned artichoke." Such articles always go on to tell you that the artichoke, turnip, Brussels sprout, or whatever is actually far more versatile than you have known until now.

Much-needed change. Reporter thinks the new government will be better than the old, but never says needed by whom and why.

Multi-disciplinary. What used to be the main characteristic of a motley crew; a mix of specialists.

Multi-talented. DEEP TRANSLATION: Untalented. John Leo explains: "... used to identify entertainers who have great pep and who perspire a lot but do nothing particularly well."

Mused. Took the person forever to answer the question.

Myriad. A fancy way of saying "many". As one critic of journalese put it after listing a number of examples "There are myriad other examples of such journalese, including the word myriad."

Myth. A notion we have been pushing for years, but we are now ready to drop.

Nail-biter. Reviewer or reporter used cliff-hanger in an earlier story. Close election counts are always nail-biters.

Natural causes. What old people die of in small towns. Large metropolitan dailies insist on specifying the fatal illness in obituaries. "The 105-year-old great grandfather had a heart condition, arthritis, diabetes, emphysema and poor hearing, but otherwise was in good health."

Near miss. An airline mishap that is actually a "near hit."

Neo. A voguish prefix for younger liberals and conservatives. It means "not quite" or, as George Will has written, "I suspect that splicing 'neo' with the sacred word 'conservative' is a form of flinching."

Nestled. Code word for rich. "The Gotrocks' home is nestled among horse farms and rolling estates." Poor folks' homes tend to "stand starkly along lonesome dirt roads."

New breed. Said of any group of younger workers, professionals or athletes. New breeds are usually ten years younger and 20 pounds lighter than the old breed.

New Hampshire. A New England state that emerges for a few weeks every four years as a place exclusively populated by political analysts. "The merest bag boy at your typical Nashua supermarket checkout counter," wrote Meg Greenfield in *The Washington Post* at the end of the 1968 campaign, "knows how to toss off a newsy, compact analysis of his feelings about the contest that does credit to both himself and his state on the 6 o'clock news." Over four decades later, this observation still applies, but is being replaced by Iowa, which is New Hampshire with corn.

Nightmare. The only metaphor that TV anchors can think of when describing an unfortunate circumstance involving a child. The accepted cliché is, "A mother's worst nightmare became reality Tuesday when..."

No easy answers. This is a caveat that reporters attach to complex subjects if they themselves haven't a clue and can't find the answer easily on Google. It's not a new way to avoid digging. In the Jan. 16, 1986, issue of *The New Republic*, Michael Kinsley checked *The Washington Post's* 1985 issues and found "no easy answers" were applied to 23 questions, including how astronauts go to the bathroom.

No explanation was offered. We forgot to ask. There was nobody there but the cleaning crew.

Nobody locks their doors. A small town or village where something bad happens and the big city reporters believe everything the guys in the diner tell them.

Noir. Reviewers' favorite for a book or film most people will find depressing as hell. "The noir story with a happy ending has never been written, nor can it be," explained Otto Penzler in huffingtonpost.com, books page, Aug. 10, 2010. Headlined "Noir Fiction Is About Losers, Not Private Eyes," Penzler concluded, "The lost and corrupt souls who populate these tales were doomed before we met them because of their hollow hearts and depraved sensibilities. I love noir fiction. It makes doom fun. And who doesn't like fun?"

Non-essential. Classification of most public employees told to stay home during major storms. However the terminology is changing as Howie Carr, *Boston Herald* columnist, wrote on Jan. 26, 2011, when a snowstorm hit New England: "Have you noticed that the hacks don't use the word 'non-essential' to describe themselves anymore? It was just a little too descriptive... people with real jobs are likely to conclude that said state employees are...not essential. So sometime either late this afternoon or early tomorrow we may be hearing on the radio or TV that the state's 'non-emergency' workforce is being given yet another day off."

Nonprofit. An organization that pays no taxes, often receives taxpayer funds, and is supposed to be doing things that the reporters and editors approve of. The designation never includes the fact that the nonprofit's top executives are paid outrageously high salaries, usually far more than the reporter or editor could dream of. If the nonprofit is disliked by the paper, it is described as industry supported, or as a liberal or conservative pressure group, or a lobbying arm, or privately financed. Top salaries are then prominently noted.

Nor'easter. New England weather journalese for any storm, even if it comes from the southwest or anywhere else. Originally a

nor'easter was a severe storm from the northeast, but that was prior to TV weather reporting.

Nosedive. Anything dropping, from the stock market to sales of last year's smart phones. Does not apply to airplanes, since reporters under 70 would not know that's where it originated.

Not clear. Reporter has no idea what happened, will happen, or what it means.

Notable. Someone or something worth noting. Famous has been used elsewhere in the story of page. "SF Symphony boasts notable fall imports," headlined *The Examiner* of San Francisco, Oct. 15, 2010. Exceptions are often notable.

Noted authority. Said of anyone on the reporter's speed-dial or Twitter feed.

Notorious. A person who has a lousy reputation and a long rap sheet who couldn't win a libel suit. Every Third World country prison is notorious.

Nude. A dead body found without clothing. It must be mentioned every time the story is rehashed. If the body is dressed, no description of apparel is necessary, unless it's a man in women's clothing, which should be repeated at every turn.

Numbers. Increasing numbers and growing numbers were explained in a classic column by *The Washington Post* Ombudsman, Richard Harwood, May 5, 1991. He gave 11 examples from his paper of "increasing numbers" (such as "increasing numbers of high school students are choosing state colleges") and 12 examples of "a growing number" (as "A growing number of people in the U.S. furniture business believe American designers should get some kind of government support.") His explanation: "The beauty of these clever literary devices, as all editors are aware, is that they relieve us of any need to quantify in numerical terms the full dimensions of the many trends we must deal with daily, whether, for example, the growing number of people favoring subsidies for furniture designers represents a leap from two to three or from a million to a billion. For the purposes of establishing a trend, precise statistics are immaterial to the journalist. Growing and increasing numbers speak for themselves." Evidently, Ombudsman Harwood spoke to himself and was not heard on the copy desk, since a search of *The Washington Post* archives of recent years reveals that the use of "increasing numbers" and "growing numbers" has not decreased. Indeed, the use may be increasing or growing.

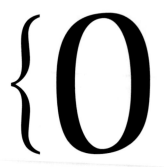

Obscure. Anything not known to the reporter before working on the story. "She was charged under the provisions of an obscure law making it illegal to bury people alive."

Official. Anyone on a city, state or federal payroll.

Old World charm. A restaurant with checkerboard tablecloths, old guys as waiters and wine sold by the pitcher. Also, a neighborhood with three or more Italian restaurants.

Olive branch. Which good guys extend and bad guys reject.

Ombudsman. The equivalent of a fullback on a football team, the ombudsman protects editors and reporters from getting tackled by readers. The ombudsman may, in his or her column, criticize his own paper's reporting, but the staff generally ignores it. The position of ombudsman is usually one of the first to be eliminated when a paper is cutting editorial costs. Although an ombudsman can be female, she is never called ombudswoman. Ombudsman is a Swedish title for an agent or representative of a trade union, political party, employer group or other association. A few Swedish papers have someone like a readers' ombudsman but under a different title, such as "quality editor."

Omnibus. This word, according to veteran newsman and writer Bill Mead, means absolutely nothing, zero, zip, nada. An omnibus crime bill is nothing more than a crime bill.

On edge. A city, community or neighborhood is "on edge" when the reporter interviewed one resident who says he or she is a bit worried while ten others say they don't give a hoot.

On the job. Working. Not to be confused with the British slang term "on the job", which the Brits would find quite an achievement in cases such as this, from *The New York Times,* Feb. 19, 2011: "The chief executive of Time Inc., Jack Griffin, is leaving the company after less than six months on the job."

On track. Plans are moving along until they get *derailed*.

Once thought to be. This is what we were saying last Wednesday when we didn't understand what was going on.

One day. Obligatory prediction in any story about scientific or medical research. As in, "The work one day might help cure kids of biting fingernails."

One of a kind. Reviewers' favorite for a film, performance or book, meaning it's so bad we hope no one else will make one like it. When used in a news story, the paper will get ten reader comments saying it's been done a dozen times before.

Only time will tell. Sign-off line beloved of television reporters covering summit conferences or unresolved municipal battles, such as, "Will the town dump continue to be open on Sundays? Only time will tell."

Operations. Murders, kidnappings or hijackings carried out by terrorists or, if they have a name like Operation Howling Moon, by the U.S. Government. Not to be confused with "procedures", which are operations done by surgeons.

Operative. Anyone getting paid to promote something or someone. Political operatives are not identified as shady, but often are.

Opportunity. A real mess. Bankruptcies, building collapses and the like are usually seen as opportunities. Worse disasters are known as challenges.

Optics. What something looks like. Optics used to be called image. Politicians are always worried about it. In a story about details of the Democratic National Convention in Charlotte, N.C., in September, the *Los Angeles Times*, on Jan 17, 2012, reported about the stadium where President Obama will hold his acceptance speech: "Party Chairman Wasserman Schultz also downplayed any optics issues linked to the Bank of America name being on the stadium, home to the NFL's Carolina Panthers."

Outdoorsman. A guy with two or more shotguns and a chainsaw. He drives a pick-up.

Outgoing. It can mean extroverted but can also have a **DEEP TRANSLATION:** A happy drunk; loud and embarrassing.

Outrage. What any gang of shouting, fist-raising demonstrators display, usually against a nation or people so far away the demonstrators can safely scream all they want.

Outspoken. Very noisy; abusive; a pain in the neck.

Overcrowded. Crowded. Always used in articles about schools, mental institutions and prisons. A group called Unicorn Hunters, which lists words that should be banned, had this in its 1985 list, with the nomination by James Knight of Nashville saying, "We have not had a simply crowded prison since 1982."

Overkill. Originally a term applied to nuclear warfare but now used for any excess no matter how piddling. The word has been so overkilled as it now is as likely to show up in the food pages— "iceberg lettuce overkill at the salad bar"—as it is in an article on the thermonuclear peril. At its overkilling-usage height it was once carried in a *Washington Times* article on "sewer overkill."

{P

Pall. A pall of gloom descends, is cast, falls or dampens when there's bad news. Also, what thick smoke creates.

Panacea. Word that is journalistically linked to a negative modifier. "It is not a panacea, he warned." Ditto for *cure-all* and *easy answers* of which there are also none.

Parade. Red flag word for people who have organized a march. Editors know that if they call an anti-abortion or pro-choice march a parade, they will get hundreds of reader responses for their choice of words, guaranteeing them fodder for the letters to the editor page. Other red flag words that have a proven ability to generate large piles of mail include apologist (for spokesperson) and drivel (for information).

Paradigm. Fancy way of saying example or model. Usually used incorrectly, unless it's in a story about language, according to its first definition: "A list of all the inflectional forms of a word taken as an illustrative example of the conjugation or declination of which it belongs," according to the *American Heritage Dictionary of the English Language*. Also, in plural, two coins worth four nickels.

Paradise. Almost always used in the negative, as "Tax Paradise Lost" or "Sweden's Socialist paradise in trouble."

Paradox. (1). Obligatory description of two facts that don't match up. "The paradox of a vegetarian big game hunter was not lost on this reporter." (2) Two doctors.

Parcel. A lot or area for a building.

Partier. A drunk.

Partisan. Someone who is not independent, but pushing his or her own agenda or project. Originally, a civilian fighter in World War II.

Pass muster. To meet some standard, often unspecified.

Passionate. Variously a person who spits when they speak or a sloppy drunk.

Paving stones. What rioters rip up and hurl at police or soldiers. Weight and size of the stones are never stated, but they must be the smallest paving stones in use, designed specifically to be torn up and hurled.

Peasants. People who inhabit the travel pages and who do folkloric things and live on "hearty soups." They do not exist in the U.S. or Canada, but populate the rest of the world.

Peccadillo. A favorite of columnists, long passed retirement age, to describe a politician's misstep that rates simply a smile and a wink, wink, nudge, nudge.

Penultimate. This word actually means next-to-last, but is beginning to show up as a word for the ultimate, epic, amazing, or super-ultimate—until someone tells the reporter it's used incorrectly.

People are saying. Reporter talked about it with the person at the next desk.

People's Republic. (1) Nation where you are shot if you disobey. (2) Extremely liberal areas, such as in the People's Republic of Takoma Park, MD or the People's Republic of Cambridge, MA.

Peppery. Short and overbearing; a real pest.

Percolate. Something is brewing or cooking and getting hotter.

Perfect storm. Reporter claims conditions are right for something to happen. Something else usually happens.

Perhaps. As in "perhaps the largest" or "perhaps the fastest". The reporter doesn't really know if it is. The reporter will get ten emails saying it's not at all the largest, fastest or whatever. Next time, the reporter will use, "It is believed to be..." This will generate more emails, most starting something like, "Anyone who believes such rubbish is an idiot."

Period of time. "What else could there be a period of?" asks Stanley Bloom, a British writer and translator. "Either 'period' or 'time' is redundant. Even then, the remaining word is sufficiently vague to allow journalists to avoid any kind of precision."

Perplexing. Something so puzzling the reporter can't figure it out or find someone to explain it. Taxes are always perplexing, since mathematics could be involved.

Personal relationship. What a naughty politician or corporate executive is caught having, but should not have, with a secretary or assistant.

Pesky. Mosquitoes, bedbugs, roaches, mice. Rats are too big to be pesky. Potholes, dog poop, noisy bars and other neighborhood problems are pesky for elected officials.

Phalanx. The crowd of photographers and reporters whom celebrities or big name criminals must face, usually outside of a courtroom.

Philanthropist. Anybody who donates a lot of money, usually at least $1 million.

Picture postcard village. Any New England village with a white church with tall steeple and a village green. Norman Rockwell will be mentioned.

Picket-fence community. Not quite a gated community, but almost. See also *Well-manicured lawns*.

Pipeline. When not referring to a real pipeline, this means something in the works, but don't bet it will be a success.

Pitched. When not referring to baseball, it's obligatory in describing a battle when "fierce" has already been used.

Pivotal. Used to describe an event the journalist figures is important, which makes the story important.

PLAT DU JOURNALESE

Below is a menu of essential ingredients found spicing up or watering down restaurant reviews and food features. Wine and booze are not included. They deserve their own dictionary of translations.

ARTISANAL. Homemade from scratch. So they claim.

AUTHENTIC. Real food, not the fake stuff.

BACKGROUND. If it doesn't refer to the noise of the place, but to the dish, maybe you can taste some ingredients if you have a good imagination.

BALANCE. Nobody knows what this really means, but an obscure FDA law requires it to be used at least once in a restaurant review. "A well-balanced Martini precedes the perfectly-balanced smoked salmon appetizer."

BIODYNAMIC. Loaded with just about everything.

CELEBRITY CHEF. A cook who was on TV with this week's reality show celebrity.

COMFORT FOOD. The kind Mom used to make, even if she were a lousy cook.

COMFORTABLE. Went down without giving you gas or heartburn. When describing the restaurant, the chair is not rickety, the table is steady on four legs and there are no loud-mouth drunks in the place.

COMPANIONS. Unless referring to the person you're with, it's food that goes well with some other food, like macaroni and cheese.

COMPLEX. Everything was thrown in.

CONVENTIONALIZE. The chef has no idea what it means, but that's how he or she describes something on the menu.

COZY. The place is so small you not only share the conversation with the people at the next table, but you can share their food if they're not looking.

DECADENT. A dessert with at least 1,000 calories.

DENSE. Thick. Refers to a dish, not a waiter or waitress, even though they may be.

DIMENSION. Something that adds something. It doesn't mean the size of the servings.

DRIZZLE. Sprinkled with.

EARTHY. If you've eaten earth as a kid, this will remind you of it.

EATERY. A blue-collar diner or café that serves better food at a third the price than the snobby restaurants reviewers fawn over.

EXECUTED. The dish was made.

EXPLOSION. What some tastes do in the mouth. No law suit is known to have been filed for mouth or teeth damaged by such a blast.

FINISH. You can taste it for two hours after.

FUSION. A mish-mash.

GENEROUS. Portions that are not in direct proportion to their price.

GENETIC. A taste, texture, flavor that's supposed to be in the dish. Also, an off-the-shelf ingredient, not a fancy brand.

GREEN. When not referring to the environment or vegetables, it means amateurs. As Jason Atherton wrote about Shanghai's Table No. 1, in *CityWeekend*, July 2010, "Unfortunately, while the food here is impeccable, the green waitstaff were infuriatingly hapless, bringing us items we never ordered and forgetting items we did order. Be sure to check the bill carefully."

GOURMET. Any dish advertised as "gourmet" means, "Don't eat it," warns Phyllis Richman, former food writer for *The Washington Post*.

HINT. Any taste that doesn't knock you off the chair.

HONEST. Unless it means the waiter didn't kite the bill, honest means that the food was actually made from what it was supposed to be made from. A dish described as honest infers that other dishes, not so named, are dishonest.

INNOCUOUS-LOOKING. Suspicious.

INTEGRITY. You can taste what it is supposed to taste like.

INSPIRATION. The chef found the recipe in an old newspaper food section. Naturally he or she won't admit it.

INVOLVE. To throw in some ingredient.

JOINT. A cute way of describing a very fancy place when it's a neighborhood favorite.

JUDICIOUS. An amount of an ingredient that doesn't ruin the dish.

LAYERS. Means whatever you imagine it might mean. "Old-world breads boast layers of taste," headlined a story about rye bread in the *Los Angeles Times*, Jan 13, 2011.

MARRIED. A dish or ingredient that lives happily with another. If they don't get along, they are not divorced but live together just to annoy the reporter.

MENUESE. The language of menus, often loaned by reporters in their reviews.

MOLECULAR GASTRONOMY. A type of cooking that requires the chef to have passed high school chemistry.

OFFENDING. It's lousy.

ORGANIC. Expensive. The insecticides, fungicides, herbicides and fertilizers the farmers use are approved as organic by their manufacturers.

PAIRING. Something goes with something.

PERFECT. The reviewer says so, so it must be so.

PLATED. Food placed on a plate.

PLAYFUL. A dish that makes you laugh.

PUCKERY. Like biting into a lemon. "Puckery bursts of contrasting flavor," wrote one reviewer.

QUAFFABLE. Wine you can serve to guests who will drink anything.

RATED. Zagat or some local magazine listed the place.

REWARDED. The reviewer got served something that tasted OK.

RIFF. Something the chef tossed together.

ROBUST. It has a taste and it's tough as hell.

SATISFYING. Nobody at the table complained. Why should they, the paper is picking up the bill.

SILKY. Obligatory description of at least one dish in an Asian restaurant.

SPIKED WITH. Something that was thrown in.

SURPRISE. A dish that doesn't look like what you ordered. It was most likely served by mistake, but the waiter insists it's the chef's own version. Also, a dish that doesn't taste like cardboard. And finally, the bill that's just about what you estimated it would be.

SUSTENANCE. Food that will keep you stuffed for a while

SWIMMING. Any object in a soup or sauce. What the bug does in countless "Fly in my soup" jokes.

TASTES LIKE CARDBOARD. Restaurant reviewers and food writers are among the very few people on earth, except teething babies, who know what cardboard tastes like. Insiders insist that Le Cordon Bleu Institute devotes a graduate-level course to this subject. A true cardboard maven should always specify exactly what kind of cardboard the dish tastes like: white mechanical pulp, recycled, double or triple corrugated, laminated, chromo imitation, boxboard, multi-ply folding, cup board, polyethylene-coated waterproof, paperboard, drawing board—to name a few cardboards of varying tang, savouries, consistencies and sensory enervation to the palate.

"Venison tenderloin with quince, root vegetables, and chestnuts, a promising sounding dish, tasted like cardboard, and the quince was indelibly hard and undercooked," according to Corby Kummer, in a review of Bistro du Midi, *Boston Magazine*, March 2010. In his book, *The Pleasures of Slow Food*, Kummer does not discuss the pleasures of cardboard.

"Head for the Cafe Car, and enjoy one of those pizzas that taste like deflated tricycle wheels while you're at it," Alex Beam, *Boston Globe* columnist, Feb 2, 2011, advised passengers planning to take the Acela train to New York. Beam may be the only living American journalist who has tasted deflated tricycle wheels and lived to write about it.

A quick Google search of "tastes like" found cardboard was tops with 718,000 hits, followed by rubber 325,000, wood 232,000, shoe leather 14,400, paper 11,700, wool 11,300, and wet wool only 510 even though millions of kids have chewed on wet wool mittens and do know what it tastes like. "Taste like deflated tricycle wheels" got seven hits, all referring to tire gourmet Alex Beam.

UBIQUITOUS. An ingredient used in every snobby restaurant in America. You'd have to move to Uzbekistan to escape it.

UMAMI. Required Japanese word in all food or restaurant articles. It's some kind of taste or savoriness. Google has 240,000 citations if you ask, "What is umami?" Check it out and you'll still be puzzled.

UNEXPECTED. A dish that gets guests asking, "What the hell is this?"

WELL-STRUCTURED. A dish that stands up all by itself.

Plaudit. Someone clapped his or her hands.

Player. When not about sports or gamblers, it means a hot-shot executive or a company.

Plummet. What the stock market does when it doesn't surge. Even though the word means to fall like a rock, this is what airplanes do when they fall.

Plump. Fat. Used only for women. Men are chubby.

Plunge. The stock market went down half a point, but stock held by the reporter went down three. When buses go off cliffs in Third World countries, they plunge.

Ply. What sailboats do in water and hookers with their trade.

Pockmarked. A commercial or industrial area with a bunch of empty buildings.

Poised. Ready for something.

Police continue to investigate. Readers and viewers certainly hope so. That's their job. It would be news if they didn't.

Political oxygen. Modish word for political talk. "Last year the same debate consumed political oxygen like a hungry fire," commented *The Philadelphia Inquirer*'s philly. com, Mar. 27, 2011.

Political surrogate. "You get to be on TV all the time. Everyone wants your opinion, and you get a good job later if you don't mess up." And if you mess up? "It's gross. They throw you under a bus." Definition by a Garry Trudeau character, in *Doonesbury*, Mar 7, 2010.

Pop icon. Rock singer who has been around for more than two years, once did something outlandish, and whose name has shown up in a newspaper outside his or her home town. "Since releasing more than 2,000 lemmings on stage during a 1982 concert, he has become something of a pop icon."

Popular hostess. Never a shortage of free loaders at her cocktail parties.

Position. To put something someplace.

Poster boy. Exemplar. One of the overworked news metaphors with a *Factiva* count of 22,867. Poster boys are often *rock stars*, which is similarly overworked. Occasionally a newspaper scores a journalese

two-bagger by employing both in the same sentence. This from *The New York Daily News,* April 3, 2011: "While many New Yorkers may not be familiar with El Sistema those who know classical music have heard of the programs poster boy, Gustavo Dudamel, the young conductor of the Los Angeles homophonic and a rock star in that world." Include "many" and the sentence scores a triple journalese.

POTUS. Shorthand for President of the United States. Steve Myers, managing editor of blog Poynter. org, noted on Sept 19, 2011, that *POTUS* was in the 1800s Philips Code for telegraphic shorthand. "*Politico* apparently is required to place it in at least one story each week," he wrote.

Power-broker. A small-town banker whose wife is related to the mayor. A state capital or Washington lawyer or lobbyist who is always available to the media.

Powerhouse. Any person or organization that has plenty of clout. Never used to identify a power generation plant.

Powerful. Guys willing to spend lots of money on politicians.

Prairie fire. Something that spreads fast, even if there isn't a prairie within thousands of miles. "The prairie fire of mass protests in Egypt continues to burn and shows signs of intensifying," Associated Press reported.

Precious. Any swamp, seashore, forest, or open land threatened by development or hit with an oil spill or a natural disaster. See also *Fragile*.

Precip. Precipitation on television news. Way back in 1986 a note from Anthony A. Spleen, a newsman for *WGAL-TV8* in

Lancaster, PA: "I have tried for years to understand why weathermen ...say 'we will be experiencing some precip today.' Is it really that difficult to say 'precipitation'?"

Precocious. A brat, usually wise beyond his or her years.

Premium. When not a give-away or a come-on, it's something pricey, as in a *premium* address.

Presence. When used to describe a person, anyone who has been around the place so long he or she is mistaken for the furniture. Can range from a janitor to a hack who always backs the right politician.

Presser. JOURNOSPEAK for a press conference.

Presumably. Codeword telling the reader that the writer is about to take a wild-assed guess.

Prestigious. Any award, even if nobody outside the recipient's family ever heard of it. Papers or journals that reporters quote from are always prestigious.

Previously undisclosed. Something that's been on file or available for years, but the reporter just noticed it.

Previously unknown group. Terrorist organization, unknown to the news writer, has claimed responsibility for a bombing.

Prickly. Anything that can get a politician, bureaucrat or business leader in trouble. "Faced with the prickly issues of being sued by his mistress while he's in a heated divorce battle, Senator Blowhard is now stressing family values."

Priors. A criminal record. Copspeak adopted by reporters.

Pristine. Any natural area threatened with development, an oil spill, fire, or other catastrophe. See also *Fragile*.

Probe. An inquiry or investigation. Veteran UK journalist Andrew Drinkwater wrote in a 2008 blog on Journalese: "My first editor said that a probe was only ever used by doctors to explore problems with bodily orifices and should never be used by a journalist other than in this context." As if the poor guy didn't get enough sticking, the *Boston Herald*, Dec 9, 2010 headlined: "Police probe Burlington man found stabbed."

Proclaim. To say. Mike Feinsilber wrote about the term in a memo to AP writers: "We tend to apply this verb to every presidential utterance, sometimes with silly results. 'We have begun to pick ourselves up and dust ourselves off, and we've begun the work of remaking America,' Obama proclaimed, but it just doesn't sound like a proclamation. In Newton, Obama proclaimed that 'once-shuttered factories are whirring back to life,' but it sounds like he more likely just said it. 'But the administration officials rejected that dealing with global warming will undermine the nation's economy, as some GOP lawmakers proclaimed.' In this (particularly hard to read) sentence, we have nameless lawmakers doing the proclaiming. Silliness approaches. In journalism, even license plates can proclaim: 'the city sought to educate the nation about its plight by introducing license plates that proclaimed 'Taxation Without Representation'.'"

Professed. The person claims something and we don't believe it, but we'll print it anyhow. As foxnews.com, in an AP story Feb. 11, 2012, reported: "Jeanette Barraza-Galindo conspicuously left her bags of teddy bears and throw pillows on a bus during an inspection at the Texas-Mexico border, and professed ignorance about the $277,556 officers found hidden inside. The bags were handed to her at a bus station, gifts to be given to a child upon her return to Mexico, she told investigators."

Profound. Big. Deep. Used by reporters and editors wanting to sound profound. "Albany madness creates an opening for profound reform," headlined a *New York Daily News* story, June 16, 2009.

Progress. Describing any claim of medical advance, such as fighting the common cold. Also accepting diplomats' claims about the results of an international meeting.

Projection. A meteorologist's guess based on a computer's guess.

Prominent. A big shot that never lets anyone forget he or she is a big shot. All doctors, lawyers, bankers and business executives, but never bus drivers, mechanics, teachers, or people from a hundred other useful occupations. Ever hear of a prominent nurse or a prominent fire fighter? No reporter ever has, either.

Promising debut. A reviewer's standard. Sam Sacks, *Wall St. Journal* columnist, explains: "The phrase has long been used by reviewers as a means of polite dismissal, the ultimate in damning with faint praise."

Protean. Nobody really knows if this is good or bad when it's used to describe someone—who can either be erratic, flighty and inconsistent or he or she can be adjustable, a jack of all trades, a renaissance man. Reporters who use the word think it's classy; the rest of us equate the use of the term to horseflies at a picnic.

Public interest. Label of an organization the reporter likes. Otherwise, it's a lobby or pressure group. Every American is comforted to know that there are thousands of lawyers, flacks, hacks and assorted others working hard in Washington for the "public interest." The organizations are usually non-profits so they pay no taxes in the interest of the public.

Public outcry. Exaggerated description of disagreement. **DEEP TRANSLATION**: Three letters to the editor or five people carrying signs outside City Hall. Outcry becomes outrage when there's a demonstration of more than a dozen people.

Pummel. What rain storms do to coasts.

Pundit. An expert who sounds smarter than an analyst, according to Boston's northendwaterfront. com blogger Matt Conti, who has met plenty of experts, pundits and analysts in his career.

Punishing. Any storm, hurricane, tornado, flood or other natural disaster. Also a military operation that the reporter doesn't approve of.

Purportedly. Fancy way of saying allegedly, supposedly or "as rumor has it...."

Pursue new challenges. The person got fired, which everyone including the reporter knows, but that's what the person says, unless it's "to spend more time with my family."

Pursue other interests. The person got fired or quit before indictments were handed down.

Putative. Columnist favorite to show off a word remembered from Latin. The writer believes something but has no idea if it's true, false, a myth or total rubbish, just don't hold him or her responsible.

Puzzling. The reporter has no idea what's happening.

Quality time. What parents spend with their families, at least when the kids aren't engrossed in some electronic game.

Quiet lives. What big city reporters say about the existences of people in small towns. If writers really want to make sure the reader gets the idea, they put people in a corner, as in *The Washington Post* headline: "Sandy Hook: Residents Lead Quiet Lives in Forgotten Corner."

Quizzed. "Asked some questions," as defined by British journalist Graeme Whitfield in his *Journalese-English Dictionary (first edition)*. He adds that it is another example of a term that would never be used in real life "I'm late, dear. I was being quizzed by my boss over that report I wrote."

Raconteur. A garrulous bore.

Rage out of control. What forest fires always do.

Ragtag. An unorganized rebel force. "Libyan rebels' ragtag army has heart but lacks organization and training," *The Washington Post* reported Mar. 31, 2011. Also applied to scruffy musicians—such as "a ragtag band of rockers."

Raise awareness. Used to describe educational, promotional or lobbying efforts by a group the reporter agrees with. It's handy for job security when the reporter knows it's a con, bunk or a rip-off, but the editor doesn't think so.

Raises questions. Reporter is wondering because he or she has no answers to questions they forgot to ask. Contributor Howard Kate adds that the reporter has learned something that no one else is concerned about yet.

Raise the specter. Reporter's own crystal ball and about as accurate.

Raise the stakes. When not gambling, it means more money or more risk, as in a development project, political campaign or labor contract negotiations.

Raise suspicion. The person is guilty, but we can't prove it yet.

Rally. A demonstration where police broke no heads. Also a way to describe a late stock market surge that earlier radio and TV reports failed to predict.

Rant. The reporter doesn't like what the person says. If he or she likes it, it's a statement.

Rare. An occurrence that hasn't been reported for a week or two. If it has, the reporter never heard of it.

Rattled. Someone is all shook up.

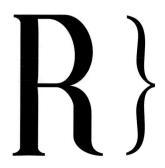

Raw data. Data that has not yet been cooked.

Reaching out. Bending someone's ear. How politicians, business executives, PR hustlers and activists push their agenda on someone else. In a story headlined "Local group aims to prevent dog violence," *The Toledo Blade*, Sept 25, 2011, reported: "A newly formed group is working to change the perception among some urban dwellers that dogs, especially 'pit bull' breeds, are good only for fighting or protection. Toledo's PET Bull Project is reaching out to dog owners and children, offering free training in city parks, education, and spay and neuter information as it tries to keep more dogs off the streets and out of fighting rings."

Reads like a Who's Who. A guest list for a charity ball.

Reality check. (1) TV reporters' introduction to a statement about something they say is real. It's anyone's guess if items not deserving a reality check are real or not. (2) What TV meteorologists do when they look out the window.

Reassigned. The person got fired, but we can't confirm it yet.

Rebrand. A marketing term now used by journalists for re-naming and giving a new look to. **DEEP TRANSLATION**: The company is doing lousy. The CEO ordered a new logo.

Recapitalization. Business writers' favorite, meaning the company is going broke and needs money fast, according to Walter Carter, financial analyst and author, who has studied more such companies that he cares to remember.

Recently. The reporter lost the press release.

Red ink. According to the business press, this always comes in rivers. It never seeps, but always gushes.

Reeling. Any neighborhood, group, town, family or political party hit with a disaster or tragedy or scandal.

Reflect. A reporter displays his erudition by saying something is similar to or the result of something else. "Slipping imports reflect slowing economy," the *Los Angeles Times* reported, Oct. 9, 2007.

Reform. Often used by journalists for change or overhaul rather than its proper use as change for the better. Mike Feinsilber of The Associated Press says this is an example of a word that may carry a meaning or connotation the writer may not have intended. He quoted AP reporter Jim Drinkard on this term:

"When folks on the Hill or in the administration want to change policy, they introduce legislation that they call their 'reform' bill. It gets called that in every statement, press release and floor speech, and pretty soon reporters start to adopt the nomenclature. But 'reform' is a loaded word.... Using it means the writer has made a judgment that the proposed changes are in a positive direction. We're now coming up on a season of 'reforms': health care, financial regulation, energy policy, and the like. We need to dust off our less-judgmental synonyms—change, overhaul, revamp, redo, update, modify, alter, shift, revise, reshuffle, shake up, adjust, amend."

Reformist. Any person with a cause that the reporter and editor support. If they don't, the person is an agitator.

Reinvent. The company is in big trouble. It's betting on a new CEO, new logo and a new color for its main product.

Rein in. A plan, bill or scheme is slowed down. Rein in is always used when something has been galloping. Young reporters think rein in means the roof leaks.

Religion. People are never simply Protestants, Catholics or Jews. They are staunch Protestants, devout Catholics and observant Jews.

Remains to be seen. All-purpose summary, with a touch of cynicism, when reporting someone's ability to keep a promise, such as, "It remains to be seen if the new governor can create the 50,000 jobs he promised."

Renowned. Well-known to somebody.

Reportedly. The word "reportedly" is journalese for "somebody else reported this before we did," wrote Rex Smith in the *Albany Times-Union*, April 24, 2011. On a more general level it can also mean that we have no idea if this is so, but it sounds good. It is grudgingly used by newspapers that got beat on a story and have no way of independently verifying it before deadline. Also a wildly improbable assertion, such as the following in *Parade* magazine: "The top-selling postcard of all time reportedly was one displaying a drawing by artist Donald McGill. A man in the picture asks, 'Do you like Kipling?' A woman responds, 'I don't know, you naughty boy. I've never been kippled.'"

Reputed. Known to all living things, as in the phrases, "reputed mafia kingpin" or "reputed underworld chieftain." It also signals that although the cops know it, they have never been able to make a case.

Residual delays. A traffic reporter favorite, meaning, "They're picking up the pieces and drivers are gawking."

Resonant. So loud the reporter figures everyone heard it. Reporting on an interview with Stephen Hester, CEO of Royal Bank of Scotland, the *BBC* on Feb 9, 2012 wrote: " 'I am not a robot,' was his resonant description of how he felt on seeing himself turned into a symbol of the alleged excesses of the banking industry."

Respected. All foreign newspapers that a foreign correspondent quotes are respected, if not highly respected. None are sleazy, rumor-filled, politically biased or totally unreliable, even if they are.

Restive. A region or country with a civil war, riots, demonstrations, strikes.

Restructuring. Business writers' echoing a corporate press release, which means the company's doing lousy, in big trouble, the boss got fired, and the new one's most urgent task is to change the logo.

Revolution. Unless it's a civil war, it's any minor change the reporter has been assigned to write about, such as "the packaging revolution" or "the revolution at the check-out counter."

Revolutionary. When not referring to a guy as a combatant with an automatic rifle trying to overthrow a government, it's an invention or development the reporter never heard before and believes what the PR guys say about it. He or she will get a dozen emails saying a similar thing has been around for years. Associated Press released a story on the paint roller, headlined: "The Revolutionary Roller: Choosing the Right Type and Size."

Revolving door. Going from a government job to a private sector job in the same field. Journalists never use a revolving door when they take a much better-paying job in public relations.

Rhode Island. Unit of geographic measurement, especially for forest fires, oil spills, droughts and other devastation over a huge area. Only Rhode Islanders, and perhaps a few Bay Staters, have the slightest idea of how large (or small) Rhode Island is. In describing the Gulf oil spill, *The New York Times* on May 2, 2010, quoted AP: "The surface area of the oil slick nearly tripled in size in roughly a day, growing from a spill the size of Rhode Island to something closer to the size of Puerto Rico according to satellite images analyzed by the University of Miami." The *Times*, however, in what should qualify for a Pulitzer nomination, went on to report the size of the slick was 1,150 square miles but expanded into the range of 3,850 square miles, according to a remote sensing specialist. The comparison was close: Rhode Island is 1,214 square miles, and Puerto Rico is 3,435 square miles.

Richly textured. Book reviewer favorite. Also useful for restaurant reviews. It can mean whatever you want it to mean.

Rigorous. A useful dramatic adverb for action a reporter forgets a person is paid to do. "Passengers who trigger an alert, and anyone who refuses to go through the scanners, will receive the rigorous frisking that has drawn sharp objections," reported *The Washington Post,* July 21, 2011, on a new NSA airport screening device.

Ripe. Something that may happen, as "The economy is ripe for a crash."

Ripple. Waters ripple quietly. Everything else is almost a Tsunami, as Associated Press reported Jan. 29, 2011, about riots in Tunisia and Egypt, "...unrest rippling across the Arab world...."

Rising tide. Something increases, even in places where there are no tides. "A rising tide: Meth use is soaring among Utahans," headlined the Salt Lake City's *Deseret News*, Nov. 17, 2004.

Risk. As a verb, the reporter guesses that something bad might happen.

Riveting. Said of potboiler novels involving submarines, nuclear weapons or serial killers. The only rivets most readers know about are on the pockets of Levi's.

Roadmap. A plan or program set by top national leaders for someone else, who usually ignores it or gets lost trying to follow it.

Rocked the city. Cycles of violence always rock a city or neighborhood.

Rocky history. A public figure or corporation about which there is a bulging clip file in the library.

Romantically involved. They're having sex.

Romp. Reviewer's standard for a book or film that's amusing, with comic characters and screwball plot. Such stories might be *engaging* but never *riveting* or *compelling*.

Rough and tumble. Local politics, which are proportionally more rough and tumble the smaller the town, city or state.

Roil. A favorite of headline writers for any protest or heated debate.

Rubenesque. Fat.

Rubicon. Once it's crossed, there's no turning back, except when it's a political promise.

Ruddy-faced. An apt description for certain complexions. **DEEP TRANSLATION**: Drunk or given to drink. *The New Statesman's*, description on Dec. 17, 2001, still applies: "British clubhouses, always built to a traditional country-mansion design, however new, are filled with ruddy-faced chaps who moan about their children wearing designer labels, but who are themselves plastered with brand names, frequently accompanied by newly minted, absolutely meaningless armorial shields."

Rugged. All mountains in which hikers are lost or where planes crash.

Rumors persist. An easy lead-in to an ongoing story about a potential sex/financial/political scandal when there is no new development. Rumors may be created by political opponents, other journalists, or, on a really slow news day, by the reporter, as long as the rumors have not been denounced and disproved to the media's satisfaction.

Run-down. Any old building, no matter its real shape, that a developer wants to take over and make a lot of money converting to luxury condos or apartments. Applied particularly to city-owned buildings.

Runyonesque. Any big city guys who resemble the 1930s wise guys, gamblers, crooks, bootleggers and hustlers who populated the columns and novels of Damon Runyon. Term used only by writers over 60, mainly in obituaries since there are no Runyonesque characters active today.

Saga. "Any story mentioned more than once in the papers qualifies for the title of 'saga'," according to Fritz Spiegel in *Keep Taking the Tabloids. What the papers say and how they say it.*

Salvo. At least two retorts, proposals, complaints or anything else. Often follows "opening."

Sassy. Description of London and New York tabloids that have celebrity gossip columnists and Washington bureaus. When Mortimer Zuckerman acquired *The New York Daily News*, he described it as "a street smart, sassy, serious journal."

Savvy. Something a *maven* is. A person with an academic title is an expert or a specialist or an authority, but never savvy.

Scandal-plagued. Term used for any public office, organization, trade union or company where at least two people have been indicted. If convicted, it's scandal-scarred.

Scary stuff or **Really scary stuff**. Pat reaction by a TV anchor to an investigative report on a consumer segment revealing, say, the fact that some fancy-named bottled water sold in the local supermarket is actually tap water from New Jersey.

Scathing. Any critical report. Always used when an elite blue ribbon panel censures politicians.

Scenic. Fishing boat harbors, seashores, mountains are scenic except when the paper supports a factory, shopping center, highway or wind turbines for the site.

Schadenfreude. Useful in big city political reporting. Frequently applied in Boston and Chicago, where the greatest joy of politicians is to see opponents in big trouble. The Irish translation of *schadenfreude* is "glee". Boston's three most popular forms of entertainment are sports, politics and revenge, with even a blog devoted to the subject: www. sportspoliticsandrevenge.com

Scheme. A plan or project the paper doesn't like. If the paper approves it, it's a highly desired development sorely needed by the community.

Scion. Offspring of a prominent family, especially one in New England with lots of old money. It helps if the scion does something scandalous.

Scoop. Jargon used mainly in derision, in the past tense. One reporter to another: "Wow, did you get scooped!"

Scorching. Temperature over 95 F. As if anyone has to be informed it's damned hot.

Scramble. What politicians do when a politician retires and his office opens up for election. People also scramble for supplies when a hurricane or snowstorm approaches.

Scribe. What reporters like to call reporters, but only in print.

Scrum. A bunch of pols battling for an office. Reporter shows off a knowledge of rugby. Short for scrummage, which is never used in a headline or story.

Scrutinize. Reporters repeat what politicians and bureaucrats insist they're doing when trying to unravel a big problem. What they are really doing is figuring out whom to blame for a major screw-up.

Scuttle. What happens to plans or projects when they are dumped.

Sea change. In comparison with the mortal wreckage that William Shakespeare portrays in *The Tempest*, this now describes the slightest movement in such things as investor attitudes or political leanings. These always "undergo."

Search for answers. Usually describing survivors or victims. Reporters' favorite when they can't be bothered to get out and ask questions that may produce answers.

Searching for clues. The cops have no leads in an investigation.

Seemed to be. Reporter thought so, but was totally wrong. Couples seemed to be in love until a vicious divorce battle. A neighbor who goes violently bonkers always seemed to be a quiet, friendly guy.

Seems. See *Appears*.

Seen as. The reporter's own view and attributed to nobody. "The mayor's firing of the indicted city hall hack was seen as an effort to keep from being indicted himself." Handy for headlines as "Religious use of pot seen as legal refuge," by *The Denver Post*, June 27, 2010.

Self-described. The person's a faker, but why risk a libel suit by saying so?

Self-styled. Adjective used when the reporter is not pleased with the role adopted by a person, organization or institution. It hints the role is phony. "Smith, a self-styled consumer advocate, has a lemon tattooed on his forehead." A letter to the editor of *The Washington Post* suggested that the newspaper's computers are programmed to write "self-styled citizen's lobby" whenever Common Cause is mentioned.

Send a message. To say something but not in plain English.

Sense of. TV anchors' favorite when they have no solid question to ask, such as "Do you have a sense of what the election outcome will mean?" A version of this was on *WCVB*, Channel 5, Boston, on May 21, 2011, "Can you express the level of excitement..."

Sensitive. All shorelines affected by an oil spill are sensitive. Unless they are *fragile* or *precious*.

Serial. Any criminal who does something twice or more, such as a serial bank robber. A serial killer is a weak-kneed description of a mass murderer. Also, Captain Crunch's assassin.

Seethe. Someone is getting mad. Mobs always seethe.

Seismic. Any change that would have been called a watershed, but watershed was already used in the story.

Seminal. This is a big deal, the start of important stuff. Eric Hosmer's joining the Kansas City Royals got this reaction by Bob Dutton, in *The Kansas City Star*, May 5, 2011: "His arrival in the big leagues, potentially, signals a seminal step in the club's rebuilding process." Some readers might be embarrassed to learn that the first dictionary definition of seminal is: "of or containing seed or semen."

Shadowy. Any very private business, secret military intelligence department or foreign defense agency the reporter doesn't like. But those the reporter approves of are valiant, patriotic and dedicated.

Sharp. Every response, reply, reaction, rebuke or condemnation is sharp, even though it's dull and wishy-washy.

Shapely. "Tabloid euphemism for a woman with big breasts," wrote Fritz Spiegel in *Keep Taking the Tabloids: What the Papers Say and How They Say It.*

Shattered. What happens to illusions, above all to **grand illusions**. A quiet town or neighborhood is always shattered when it's the scene of a violent crime.

Shock. Condition that sweeps a neighborhood or town when a reporter interviews two people who say, "Gee, whiz, that never happens here."

Shock waves. Reporters have built-in seismic meters that sense tremors anywhere in the globe. "Shock waves could be felt throughout the drilling community when President Obama announced a six month moratorium on offshore drilling," reported the *Hartford Courant*, June 22, 2010. Hartford, in Connecticut, is about 1,500 miles from the closest offshore oil drilling. Also, what shakes up a sleepy town when something happens. "Our exclusive report, revealing that the mayor put his cousin on the payroll, sent shock waves through this tightly-knit town." Of the ten people who read the story, two said, "Yeah, so?" and the other eight turned to the sports page.

Shovel-ready. A project waiting for public financing.

Shrill. The ultimate political put-down, often of women. The woman talks too much and is not waiting her turn.

Shroud. What snow does to an area when it's a huge nuisance. Otherwise, particularly before Christmas, snow creates a winter wonderland.

Shudder. Reporter knows that people are so worried they're trembling. "Subways don't come cheap, and the possible $4.4-billion price tag is sending shudders through City Hall," reported columnist Brian Ashton in *The Toronto Sun*, Mar 1, 2011. Shudders are often transmitted down spines, but sometimes up them.

Shutter. To close up or shut down. Reporters prefer to use "shutter" when writing about the possibility of a newspaper's being killed. It's superstition, as if plainly writing, "The paper's going to be killed," will actually kill the paper. It's the journo version of fans or radio or TV reporters jinxing a no-hitter by saying out loud that a pitcher has a no-hitter underway.

Sifted. Investigators sift through wreckage, even if they use bulldozers and back-hoes.

Sigh of relief. What people breathe when there's finally some good news, which can range from world economics to Twinkies. *Bloomberg Business Week* ran an AP story Feb. 10, 2012, saying, "Investors had breathed a sigh of relief Thursday after Greek Prime Minister Lucas Papademos and the heads of the three parties backing his government agreed to private sector wage cuts, civil service layoffs and cuts in government spending." But of far more importance to millions of Americans was a story a month earlier, as reported in the thedailybeast.com about the bankruptcy of Hostess, maker of Twinkies: "While we can all breathe a sigh of relief that our beloved sweet and oily treat will continue to be sold at a convenience store near you...."

Sign. Another way of offering the reporter's own opinion. When used with "probably" it's a double, as this AP line in a story from Tripoli, July 2, 2011: "Khadafy spoke from an unknown location, probably a sign of concern over his safety."

Signal. As a verb, something may happen. Otherwise, it's a significant occurrence or a sign of something. "Wedding rings are a signal of love," reported the *Cleveland Plain Dealer*, May 18, 2011.

Signal figure. A big-shot who calls a reporter by his or her first name.

Signature. Something a person is so famous for the reporter has to remind readers, such as Mitt Romney's signature Massachusetts healthcare law. See also **Trademark**.

Simpler times. Fifteen years before the writer was born.

Singular. Nothing like it, or at least the reporter thinks so. *The New York Times* on Feb 21, 2011, described Libya as "a singular, quasi nation."

Sinuous. Obligatory word in a headline of a story about a lost pet snake.

Sixties style. No one in the 60s wore anything but long hair and beads.

Sketchy. Reporter doesn't know what the heck is going on.

Skyrocket. Verb for what happens to costs, mostly on public projects.

Slack-jawed. Description of an amazed, surprised or just plain dumb-struck person. Used by reporters who also write mysteries.

Slash. A company cuts costs by firing workers. Politicians cut the budget by more than two percent.

Sleepy little town. One that is never, ever the scene of a steamy divorce with titillating details jolting the community. Nor is there ever a brazen bank robbery, punctuated with gunfire and causing a high-speed chase. Local teen-agers call it Dullsville.

Slew. The reporter can't figure out the exact number, but there are more than two.

Smoke-filled rooms. Where politicians in the old days met to plot and scheme. The rooms and politicians are still there, but smoking is prohibited.

Snarl. Traffic and transport are all screwed up. People are never reported as snarling at each other, even though they do.

Sobering. This is going to wake you up even if you never drink or are already sober.

Sodium. Term for salt and its bad effects, when written about in newspaper food sections. Salt, on the other hand, is used when raving about salt-encrusted rib roast. Similarly red meat is negative while "rare, thinly-sliced beef" is fine in a restaurant rave.

So-called. Anything that is "so-called" is bogus and contemptible. The one doing the calling, of course, is the media.

Soft-spoken. Introverted. **DEEP TRANSLATION:** In reference to politicians, Russell Baker wrote in *The New York Times* in 1972, "It means 'evasive,' 'mumbling,' 'wooly-headed,' and in some cases, perhaps, 'drunk'."

Solon. Handy headline word when legislator is too long, pol too short and hack too accurate.

Some say. Opinion that might possibly be supported by one quote or source, but is more likely to be the reporter's own view. A search of *The New York Times* for the 12 months ending May 25, 2011, turned up over 10,000 citations of *Some say*... Our search did not break down how many were direct quotes or in op-ed pieces or letters. See *Many*.

Some observers. Plural noun given to contradictory opinion in news stories. Meg Greenfield, in *The Washington Post*, Nov. 6, 1984, wrote a classic definition that's still true: "Some Observers is a fellow who is forever 'thinking,' except when he occasionally 'feels.' But whichever it is that day, there is one thing you can always count on with him. He is fearless. Some Observers never think or feel what others, in particular those trying to have their way in a news story, think or feel or have the gall to assert as a simple fact. His role is that of unfailing contradictor." Greenfield refuses to say who *some observers* is, but admits that "I have occasionally cited him myself."

Sophisticated. Anything complex the reporter or editor doesn't fully understand and can't explain in a story, as in "sophisticated manufacturing techniques."

Sorely missed. Someone at the bar will ask, "Wonder what happened to old Joe? Haven't seen him in a month."

SOURCE SORCERY

Sources are the fuel, food, the very lifeblood of journalism. They are a great army of unnamed people who either want to leak newsworthy information or are deathly afraid of publicity. There are sources all over the place: in police departments, Congress, the executive branch, city halls, the courts, saloons and businesses. Sometimes "sources" are really a flack and a hunch.

There are as many specific types of sources as an imaginative reporter can rely on and quote. With rare exceptions they are not identified by name. Otherwise, they would be, "John Smith, the Governor's driver, who whispered..."

Well, who are these anonymous people who feed, energize and give life to the media? Here is a small collection and definitions of sources—well-known, well-loved and well-employed by the news trade.

ANALYST. A source in the guise of a serious thinker, especially useful to quote anonymously in business and political stories.

AUTHORITATIVE SOURCE. The person got a Ph.D and won't let anyone forget it. If quoted, the reporter must give the person's full academic title and must mention that he or she has written several "exhaustive" studies on the subject.

CANNOT BE INDEPENDENTLY CONFIRMED. Said of a rumor that is so juicy that it cannot be left out of the story.

COLORFUL OBSERVER OF THE LOCAL SCENE. A source as defined by Joe Goulden when this collection was first started a quarter of a century ago: "The asylum outpatient who lives on the courthouse steps, drinks wine by the half-gallon, and, since he does not read newspapers, will not object if a reporter credits him as the source of the particularly pithy quotation needed to give life to a story about the tax assessor's office."

CONTACT. Anyone the reporter knows and who will talk about something or someone. Contacts are never identified as contacts, but if their information is used, they become any one of the various types of anonymous sources. Reporter Mick McGovern, writing in the *New Statesman*, Sept. 6, 1996, had this description: "I hadn't seen my friend for five years... I shouldn't even call him my friend, because he's not. He's a 'contact' with whom I'm friendly, which—translating from journalese—means that we got on amicably in 1991 when he helped me secure a story. I'll call him Richard."

EXPERT. The only person a reporter can find who has an answer and sounds like they know what they're talking about, even though they don't. PR companies, lobbyists, trade associations all have a stable of "experts" ready to feed a line to reporters.

FIGURE. Could be anyone. As The Associated Press reported on Nov 28, 2011, "A senior Hamas figure...."

FIXER. A local hustler, translator, door-opener, or cousin of the president, who is a necessary paid assistant to foreign correspondents working in third world dictatorships. He is never identified as a "fixer", but is often cited as "a well-informed source" or "highly knowledgeable official."

HIGHLY-PLACED SOURCE. Anyone who has a job one pay-grade above that of a college intern.

INDEPENDENT SOURCES. They often "confirm" facts. An independent source is supposedly worth much more than a plain old source or one "close to the Administration."

INDUSTRIAL OBSERVER. A corporate public relations person who took the reporter to lunch.

INFORMANT. A snitch, stoolie. Might be "highly reliable" but don't bet on it.

INFORMED SOURCES. When at a news scene, other reporters who got there first. Often, politicians leaking something they haven't the guts to say publicly. Of course, a reporter would not admit using material from an uninformed source.

INSIDER. Anyone who isn't an outside observer

NOT AUTHORIZED TO SPEAK. Classic excuse for using an anonymous source. The person is either lying or telling the truth, possibly some or both.

NOT MADE PUBLIC. The reporter got an early copy of the press release.

OUTSIDE OBSERVER. Anyone who isn't an insider.

RELIABLE SOURCE. The person on the next stool at the bar. This is the appropriate name of a watering hole at the National Press Club in Washington. Reliable sources are often highly reliable, usually reliable, very reliable or given other reinforcement. Unreliable sources are those used by competing media.

RESPECTED AUTHORITY. Never been indicted or accused of plagiarism.

SENIOR ADMINISTRATION OFFICIAL. Anyone in the White House who will talk on the promise of anonymity. When a source, it means the person is one pay scale above that of an entry clerk.

Senior officials can be as young as the reporter's grand-children.

SOURCES CLOSE TO. This could range from the mayor's driver or Mitt Romney's hair stylist.

SOURCE CLOSE TO THE SITUATION. A favorite of ESPN, which means someone who is on the same continent, says reporter Paul Hagey.

SOURCES SAY. This generally refers to the person or persons sitting across from the reporter in the newsroom.

SPECIALIST. Anyone who read a book on the subject or knows how to find an answer on Google. Often, it's a reporter on the staff who did a story about it five years ago.

THINKER. An imaginary person among intellectuals, academics and experts who say what the reporters would like to have them say. A thinker wears a bow-tie, puffs a pipe and if he stopped thinking long enough he might say something wise.

THOUGHTFUL OBSERVERS. The same as observers, this breed of source is especially astute. Usually, it is the writer himself or his or her friends. Having searched the Nexus computerized data base, Michael Kinsley of *The New Republic* found 19 "thoughtful observers" in *The New York Times* from 1977 to 1985, and 12 in *The Christian Science Monitor*. A late-May, 2011, Google search got 45,400 hits. Reliable sources say that most thoughtful observers have been sources at one time or another.

TIGHT-LIPPED. The person isn't talking. Reporter can't even find an anonymous reliable source and will be forced to use the old, dependable *SOME SAY*...

UNCONFIRMED SOURCES. They are not reliable sources, but here's what they say anyhow.

UNIMPEACHABLE SOURCE. Anyone other than the President or a Federal judge, the only two offices from which the holder may be impeached according to the U.S. Constitution. This is a point made by Joseph Goulden, who has interviewed those only unimpeachable sources during his years as a Washington reporter.

VETERAN COURTHOUSE OBSERVERS. The observer is the reporter himself, because, as Joseph Goulden explains, "the city editor will not permit him to state something of common knowledge on his own unattributed authority." Variations abound, including "veteran city hall observers," "veteran Congress watchers" and "long-time White House observers."

WATCHER. An observer who is at least 2,000 miles from his or her subject of interest. Moscow-watchers are found in Washington while Mexico-watchers may be watching from the University of Maine. As sources, if they are academics, they will insist on being quoted by name and title, with their latest book mentioned.

Spate. More than one. Sounds better than two or three. Usually refers to crimes, as spate of violence.

Spawn. Headline writer's classic verb for "create" or "cause" and perhaps even once in a writer's career is used in reference to fish eggs.

Speak out. A plug for a coming story or TV report. Someone in the news because of big trouble has granted an interview with a friendly reporter.

Speak to. New Age jargon. "No

one asks their guests to comment," says Washington researcher Susanne Berger. "Instead, they say, 'Can you briefly speak to that?'" She wishes the media would speak to readers and viewers in plain English.

Speak to the issue of. A pompous way of saying what something is about. As in, "The mayor will speak to the issue of potholes."

Specter. What's raised when something happens that the reporter thinks might cause something worse to happen. If the worse does not happen, people always breathe a sigh of relief. The reporter never mentions it was his or her earlier story that scared the hell out of readers.

Speculation. A rumor or wild guess. Associated Press, Feb. 22, 2011, reported that "the Mubarak family's wealth—speculation has put it anywhere from $1 billion to $70 billion..." The reporter evidently did not ask the obvious follow-up questions: "Do I hear 75? Anyone for 75?"

Spew. When volcanoes erupt, they spew lava. When politicians erupt, they spew venom.

Spike. To jump up. Oil prices always spike.

Spin doctor. Jargon for a flack whose spin is quoted by reporters even though they know it's spin.

Spinster. Although it may he correct to thus describe any unmarried woman, its old maidish reputation infuriates everyone to whom it is applied. One reader told *The Washington Post* it was "the most offensive, hateful word in the whole English language."

Sprawling. Any suburb, real estate development, factory or mall that the reporter doesn't approve of. Mansions are almost always sprawling. "In fact, in news stories almost anything big is sprawling," Mike Berry wrote in the *Orlando Sentinel*. "In this newspaper, the word has been applied to everything from a Las Vegas hotel to Jack Nicholson's home."

Spry. Active DEEP TRANSLATION: Any senior citizen who is not in a wheelchair or coma, as defined in John Leo's *Time* essay on "Journalese for the Lay Reader."

Staggering. When not referring to a drunk or someone bopped on the noggin, it means a large number, at least large to the reporter but probably peanuts in a state or federal budget or to a corporation or politician. The *Boston Herald*, reporting on presidential candidate Mitt Romney's campaign expenses for three months ending June 30, 2011, noted $64,000 for travel "aboard a 2005 Cessna Citation CJ3, an eight-seat luxury corporate jet with leather interior and a staggering $5.8 million price tag."

Stake out. To grab a piece of property or a group of voters or a special market. Not to be confused with a police stakeout.

Stalled. It's held up for some reason beyond the understanding of the journalist. Justin G. Friedman, who knows the doings of Washington, DC, says stalled is often used in legislative context, as "The measure was passed by the House but remains stalled in the Senate."

Star. Every person who once got a job as an extra in a Cecil B. DeMille "cast of thousands" film. Also used to describe a former high school athlete, who may have played one year on the fourth squad of a team, when he or she does something newsworthy.

Star-crossed. Said of the Kennedys. Other examples of Kennedy Journalese include frequent use of the term "dynasty", describing their buildings at Hyanniport as a "compound," and, when one of the "clan" gets in trouble, overblown lines like, "The shimmering legacy of Camelot grew slightly dimmer yesterday when it was revealed that ..." When Patrick Kennedy (D, Rhode Island) left Congress at the end of 2010, after there being a Kennedy in Congress since 1947, it was, of course, the *end of an era.*

Staring down the barrel. Someone caught at something. Not to be confused with shooting fish in a barrel.

Startling / Stunning upset. We picked the losers.

Staunch. Term for an observant Protestant. In journalese the word "devout" is reserved for observant Catholics while observant Jews are called observant Jews. A January 27, 2007, letter to the *Times of London*: "Sir, Several times recently I have seen and heard Ruth Kelly described as a 'staunch Catholic'. It seems that journalists no longer have a grasp of journalese, the language of their trade. They should be reminded that, whereas Protestants may be staunch, we Catholics are always 'devout'. ALAN MCLOUGHLIN, Helston, Cornwall." See *Religion*. Also a politician who hasn't switched opinions in the past few weeks.

State of the art. This was first used to describe any machine or gadget that did not have a vacuum tube in it or come in a wooden case, but now means anything that is not old fashioned. William Rabe, a professor who has specialized in over-used terms, reported that he has heard it "applied to everything from garbage cans to contraceptives."

Step up. Usually, something that someone else should do. A *Boston Globe* editorial of June 10, 2010, urged: "On summer jobs, both business and Government must step up." It did not mention how many summer jobs the *Globe* offered, if any.

Stern warning. What the superpowers issue to each other when air space has been violated.

Still another delay. Broadcast news term for a glitch in a rocket launch schedule that keeps reporters, camera and sound people on time-and-a-half.

Stockpile. What the superpowers do with nuclear weapons and Hamas and Hezbollah do with missiles aimed at Israel.

Storied. Reporter really doesn't know what the person or place is "storied" about, but some old person said the person or place was famous once.

Storm. Every TV weather staff has the name "storm" in it. Even if they forecast the most beautiful weather the region has ever had, it is still reported by the "Storm Team" or "Storm Center" or "Storm Watch" or some such similarly-named storm-loving bunch.

Straddle. Something that's on both sides of a property or town line. What courageous politicians do.

Straits. Usually dire. When a company is in "severe financial straits" it's about to go down the toilet.

Strategist. A hustler who knows how to raise money or get votes for a politician.

Strat comm. JOURNOSPEAK for strategic communications, which means flacking a specific cause, company, product, politics or whatever. Although it may sound like a hot new concept, the blog www.idea.org, in defining the term in 2011, wrote: that in a 2005 press release, the University of Missouri School of Journalism boasted: "Founded in 1908, the Missouri School of Journalism has set the standards for journalism and strategic communication training for almost a century."

Stress test. They'll keep trying something until it busts.

Striking. Any large or tall building the reporter likes. Otherwise, it's hulking. Also, a tall elegant woman.

Strikingly. The reporter figures you may not notice it unless you're told, as "...the two sides took strikingly different positions."

Street value. The fantastic dollar value of drugs seized in a police raid. If all these estimates were added together for a year, they would exceed the GDP for all of North America and the European Union combined.

Strong. Useful headline adjective to describe the local team that did not fare well in a tournament. "Middletown Hoopsters Finish a Strong Sixth in Holiday Tourney."

Strongly worded. Any letter or statement by a politician or public official that is written in plain English and includes demands the reporter approves of. If not, it's a harangue.

Strongman. A dictator with an army. He obviously wouldn't be a weak man to rule as he did.

Structure. Public relations speak, means to plan something. Not to be confused with a building.

Struggle to come to terms with. What people do after a mishap.

Struggling. Any company or project in trouble. The kind of defense or battle put up by politicians, organizations or rebels in a minority.

Studies show. Reporter has found a study that supports his story.

Study. A report based on interviews of at least three people and contains a page-long list of references.

Stunning. A development in a story that the reporter never thought about before he heard of it. Also, on style or fashion pages, any tall woman.

Stymied. Stuck, puzzled or totally confused. Patrick Garvin, a *Boston Globe* infographic artist, says he sees "stymied" only in news stories, and it's one of his favorites because, "it suggests it was inserted by a grizzled, curmudgeonly copy editor who remembers the days when reporters smoked and drank at their desks."

Substance. Drugs, but not the kind for curing an illness. Substance is usually abused.

Substantive. This is the real stuff. The rest of the story is unimportant.

Suggest. What medical or scientific studies indicate but can not be proved. See also **Further studies are needed**.

Suggested. Reporter has no idea of what an event or action really means and can't be bothered to find out. "...a move that suggested the attack was premeditated by his political team." Also, judicious for "said" as columnist John Kass wrote in the *Chicago Tribune,* June 3, 2011: "A few reporter friends of mine have suggested that the federal prosecutors are all so pasty and pale and humorless that they could pass for vampire hunters."

Summit. Any meeting attended by people above the clerical or secretarial level.

Survive. Handy word for tips about doing something, usually not at all risky to health, such as surviving final exams or surviving Black Friday sales. But sometimes it's serious. "Survivor's Guide for the Affluent" was the headline of an article in the May 11, 2009, issue of *Forbes*. The subhead: "Uncle Sam wants your money, and the crowd outside the gate wants your head. How to survive the populist revolt against affluence."

Suspicion. Reporter thinks something is fishy but has no proof. The *New Scientist*, July 1, 2010, headlined a story: "Gulf oil spill: Are dispersants not so bad after all?" And then added: "Suspicion of BP, meanwhile, remains high."

Swag. Gifts, food, gadgets and goodies handed out by companies at press conferences, trade shows or media events. Attendees to the Academy Awards get the loot packed in designer "swag bags." Donna Terek, *Detroit News* columnist, explained the freebie feasting at the 2011 North American Auto Show: "For many experienced show attendees, it's all about the swag, the Stuff We All Acquire, or as the folks in the press room say, "the stuff we all get."

Sweeping. More than one, such as "sweeping corruption indictments." Historic novels are usually sweeping.

Systemic. The way they've always been doing things. When it involves politics, it's usually lousy at best or criminal at worst.

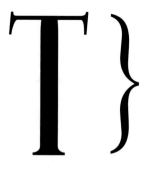

Tailspin. What something goes into when it falls, often spiraling down. Few reporters have ever seen a real tailspin except in air shows, and the planes usually pull out.

Take a look. TV anchors' command to viewers to watch something he or she just told you about.

Talking heads. What PBS believes makes fascinating TV news programs.

Tangled web. A couple of lies. The reporter will show off he was not asleep in English Lit 101, and throw in the entire line, "Oh, what a tangled web we weave, When first we practice to deceive," and then attribute it to Shakespeare. A dozen readers will immediately email the paper to say it was by Sir Walter Scott, in his poem *Marmion*. Not to be confused with the World Wide Web, on which there are a few tangles.

Tarmac. The air terminal paving on which planes are parked. But it's not Tarmac, a trade-marked bituminous pavement binder. "Tarmac has not been used in airports for over 40 years," says Capt. Larry Beck, Continental Airlines pilot, who wishes reporters would spend their time waiting at the gate or ramp to get the terminology right.

Task force. What regular folks call a committee, but usually just as inefficient or useless.

Tastefully furnished. It looks like it cost plenty, but the writer wouldn't know Chippendale from Chip 'n Dale.

Team. Used by CEOs and giant retailers to mean employees. It has been picked up by reporters referring to politicians' hacks, flacks and coat-holders. Quoting CNN, New Hampshire's *Concord Monitor* on May 19, 2011, reported: "One Republican source... tells CNN the governor's team understands a decision must happen."

Team player. A yes man on a team.

Tease. TV jargon for a lead-in to a commercial break that is supposed to keep viewers from hitting the remote to switch channels. Peter Jennings is credited with the classic tease on Dec. 15, 1992: "When we come back, Doctor Kevorkian helps two more people commit suicide."

Tectonic. What big changes or shifts are, at least according to the reporter. Rarely refers to its dictionary definition of pertaining to construction or building or, in geology, pertaining to, causing or resulting from a structural deformation of the earth's crust.

Teeming. What populations are on shores of Third World countries. Emma Lazarus's Statue of Liberty poem, "The New Colossus", calls them "The wretched refuse of your teeming shore...."

Telling. A moment or event that the reporter must inflate since he's writing about it. See also *Defining*.

Temple. When not a Jewish or Mormon or other religious place of worship, it's a school, research center, library or other facility the writer feels deserves wide admiration and respect, as in a "temple of science."

Tens of thousands. Raymond Nelson, professor emeritus of Northwestern University's Medill School of Journalism, says this has become a standard unit of measurement. "But how many are tens of thousands?" he asks, and he'd retroactively flunk any former student caught committing this reporting sin. He'd have a few candidates if they work at his old home town papers. In the year ending May 28, 2011, the *Chicago Tribune* reported "tens of thousands" 380 times and the *Sun-Times* had 113. Nelson points out that "emeritus" simply means you're retired. "It's not an honor," he says.

Testy. Bitchy. "At a testy hearing in a London courtroom, both sides traded pointed remarks yesterday about the quality of the justice system in Sweden," reported The Associated Press Feb 9, 2011, on the extradition case of Julian Assange, the WikiLeaks boss.

The question is. TV news reporter favorite ending of a story, when he or she doesn't know what will happen next.

The street. Public opinion in an Arab country. The opinion is most likely that of two "informed observers", usually taxi drivers who were the only guys the foreign correspondent could find who spoke some English. When not referring to an Arab population, it can be Wall Street or Fleet Street or Main Street.

Thirty / 30. JOURNOSPEAK for the end of story. Origin is from the Phillips Code, a shorthand for filing telegraph news, developed by Walter Phillips in the late 1800s. By extension the old school way of

saying that a journalist has passed away.

This is. Personal pronoun on radio and TV. "This is Penny Poobah reporting from the capitol" instead of "I am Penny Poobah reporting...."

Threatened. A country with a hostile neighbor. A dictator with a hostile population.

Throng. No idea how many people are there, but there are a whole bunch of them.

Thrown under a bus. In some societies, a martyr. In ours, a politician who takes the rap. See also *Political surrogate*.

Thumbs up. Cliché for something has been approved. One of the terms singled out in the *Reuters Handbook of Journalism* as journalese and to be avoided.

Tied to. Connected, but the reporter wants to hedge it a bit. Sometimes it's closely-tied. See also *Linked*.

Tight-knit. All small towns or neighborhoods in which there's a tragedy. Often the "tight-knit" community's residents are in a pitched battle over local politics, barking dogs, parking, noisy parties or zoning permits.

Time will tell. TV reporter has absolutely no idea what's going to happen but needs a line to finish with.

Tipping point. When not referring to the gratuity on a restaurant bill, it's when something is about to crash or turn into a gigantic fiasco.

Tit for tat. Revenge. Cute way of describing soldiers shooting back after the other guys shot first. When a reporter happens to be anywhere nearby, it becomes, "A murderous exchange of deadly heavy fire." Also, when one nation or politician retaliates, but without any shooting.

Titan. Big. Monstrous. Huge. But don't mention the Titanic. "Technology titans Nokia and Microsoft are combining forces to create smart phones that might challenge rivals like Apple and Google," reported The Associated Press, April 12, 2011, evidently deciding that Apple and Google do not qualify as titans.

Tonight. Expression used by TV news to "update" a story that happened in the morning. "Police tonight had no clues to this morning's grapefruit heist."

Tony. High-priced, fancy, as in "the toniest suburb."

Toddler. Reporter doesn't know exactly how old the little kid is.

Topple. What happens when a dictator is overthrown, frequently replaced by another dictator.

Tortuous. Anything complicated that the reporter can't be bothered to explain. It's also a useful word to jazz up a story. The website of KSPR TV, of Springfield, MO, June 29, 2011, had this headline: "Devil in disguise: One baker's tortuous odyssey to mastering angel food cake."

Tough minded. Journalese for stubborn. "As a general rule of thumb," Russell Baker observed in 1972, "any person described in political journalese as 'tough minded,' 'level headed' and 'realistic'—all in one paragraph—can be safely regarded as a man who would make Attila the Hun, by comparison, seem like a 'bleeding heart.'" This rule still applies.

Tourist. Person who ends up in the wrong places, such as "tourist traps," and who always over tips. Most Sunday travel sections address the reader as a traveler.

Towering. Anyone at least six inches taller than the reporter; also applied to debt and deficit. Any building higher than those nearby.

Trade barbs. Political opponents saying nasty things, some truthful, about each other, when they lock horns. Not to be confused with girls swapping Barbie Dolls.

Trade fire. Guys shooting at each other.

Trademark. Something a politician or public figure is recognized for, as a grin, necktie, haircut. Essential for political cartoonists, such as Mitt Romney's Bryl-Creamed coiffeur.

Tragedy. Death

TRAGIC CASE (STUDY)

Guy Keleny of *The Independent* (UK) lambasted this term in a news item from his own newspaper: "Corin Redgrave, the eminent stage and screen actor, who was a member of Britain's most illustrious acting dynasty, has died aged 70, his family announced yesterday. As the uncle of the late actress Natasha Richardson, who died last March after a skiing accident, this is the second tragedy to hit the Redgrave family in the just over (*sic*) 12 months."

Keleny commented on April 10, 2010: "What is going on is a bad outbreak of journalese, centered on the word 'tragedy' which is journalese for 'death'. As so often, the function of a journalese word is to create drama by setting up a phoney relationship between unrelated events. ...You could reasonably call Natasha Richardson's death a tragedy. But there is nothing remotely tragic about the death from natural causes of a man aged 70, after a life of many achievements. Everybody would have liked him to live longer, but in the end death comes for us all, and there is no more to be said."

"Why mention Natasha Richardson at all?" he asked "Thirteen months is a stretch for the 'acting dynasty in 'double-death tragedy' angle. One suspects that the reference to her may have been shoved in by a hasty editorial hand, eager to include anything of possible interest, regardless of relevance. For the second sentence of that paragraph is a mess. "A tragedy indeed."

Transparency. Howie Carr, *Boston Herald* columnist, wrote on Feb. 13, 2011, that when promised by a politician, transparency is: "Another hack buzzword meaning ... nothing."

Treacherous. Any cliff, rocky shores, waters where ships go aground and other places where careless people or daredevils get injured or killed. Rarely used to describe dictators, tyrants, despots or terrorists.

Tree-lined street. Any street, although always a street in a neighborhood with *well-manicured lawns*. Columnist John Leo writes, "In the whole history of American journalism, fewer than twenty streets have failed to be identified as tree-lined."

Trend. Anything happening that the reporter figures nobody noticed yet. Media blogger Jim Romenesko, writing that perhaps there's a trend story about Boomers wanting to visit their old college dorm rooms, commented, "Maybe there's a trend story there. Or maybe it's a 'bogus trend story.' (*New York Times* columnist and Marquette alum Gail Collins wrote in 1998 that 'an old newsroom joke is that three examples make a trend.')"

Trending. A word or topic that's getting more popular, especially on social media sites, and computed by Big Brother somewhere in cyberspace.

Trendy. Expensive and popular, especially among the young.

Troll. Inspectors, particularly parking meter checkers, troll to catch violators. Fishermen do the same to catch fish.

Troubled. The psychological condition of young criminals, teen-agers, drop-outs or guys in divorces. A region or nation can be troubled by all kinds of bad stuff, like war, terrorism, narcotics, corruption, lousy finances, poor crops. And it's always someone else's fault.

Trounce. Headlinese for sports or voting results, especially when the home team or the editor's favorite pol does the trouncing.

Try. Key word in Lifestyle sections, often tied to suggestions for leading a fuller life. "Try inviting 52 complete strangers to dinner, and watch friendships flourish."

Twisted wreckage. Place from which survivors emerge miraculously.

Typical household. Any group of 2.69 people living under the same roof.

Unabashed, unflinching, unfaltering. Jeff Jacoby, *Boston Globe* columnist, on June 21, 2010, explained: "But Saramago wasn't a Nazi, he was a communist. And not just a nominal communist, as his obituaries pointed out, but an 'unabashed' (*Washington Post*), 'unflinching' (AP), 'unfaltering' (*New York Times*) true believer." Politicians are more frequently "unabashed liberal" (41,300 hits in Google) than an "unabashed conservative" (with 15,000 hits).

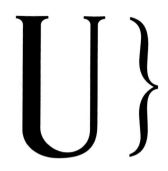

Unclear. The reporter has no idea whatsoever of what's happening.

Unconfirmed. It may not be true, but we wanted to print this before the opposition did.

Under fire. Being criticized, challenged, investigated or indicted. Never used by any war veteran unless referring to someone under gunfire.

Under investigation. Being investigated. "Under" hints at digging up dirt.

Underlined. When something is emphasized, even if it's spoken or when written and not actually underlined.

Underpinning. The foundation or basis of something, but rarely referring to what's holding up a building, bridge or other structure.

Uneasy truce. Cessation, more or less, of hostilities between warring states or celebrity couples, certain to resume after the holidays. A state that exists between the press and most of its subjects, such as the Pentagon, city hall, the Senate, Congressmen.

Unencumbered. Not burdened with something, particularly a politician without a police record or sex scandal. Tom and Ray Magliozzi, hosts of the PBS call-in show, *Car Talk*, frequently mention being "unencumbered by the thought process."

Under-reported. We missed it the first time and now, in hindsight, we should have mentioned it.

Unexpected. We told you yesterday that this wouldn't happen.

Unforgiving. Cold, wind, heat, storms.

Unparalleled. Reporter can't think of anything like it. A dozen emails will inform her or him it's as common as dirt.

Unprecedented. That which has not happened recently; not in our files.

Unquestionably. Something the reporter figures someone might not question, but readers unquestionably will do so. A favorite of editorial writers, columnists and bloggers. Robert Robb, columnist of *The Arizona Republic*, assured readers on June 17, 2008, "But the fight in Afghanistan unquestionably continues." Four years later, he can unquestionably say that again.

Unsubstantiated. It's a rumor, but with that label, we can print it.

Unsuspecting. People who generally get themselves in trouble by doing something dumb, as "The unsuspecting Miami tourist, who went hiking on a New Hampshire mountain, was found yesterday in ten-foot snowdrifts."

Up to. Reporter has no idea what the real number is but someone mentioned a big figure, like the mythical, "Up to 90 percent of start-ups fail in their first year."

Upscale. Expensive and/or excessive. Often paired with the term "baby boomer" is how Paul Dickson defined this term in 1985. A quarter century later Mike Feinsilber was dismissive of the term, asking, "Is nothing expensive any more?"

Upwardly mobile. Ambitious, aggressive, and/or obnoxious.

USA. An elusive individual American featured in stories in *USA Today*. "USA Wants Ticket to Miss Liberty Extravaganza" and "USA's Health Kick Needs More Oomph."

Vanguard. In the forefront, at least the reporter thinks so.

Vaunted. Usually used to mean highly regarded or acclaimed, even though the dictionary says it means boastful or bragging.

Venerable. Anything or anyone over 59 that the reporter likes and who has not been involved in a major scandal. A person with only a few enemies.

Viable. Workable in the abstract. Applied to options and alternatives.

Vie. What politicians do when running for office or teams do when trying to win a championship.

Virtual. A filler word that is usually used in the exact opposite meaning of its *American Heritage Dictionary* definition: "Existing or resulting in essence or effect though not in actual fact, form, or name." For example, Blain Kamin wrote in the *Chicago Tribune*, June 23, 2010: "When the plaza at the Trump International Hotel & Tower reached virtual completion in May, I wrote that it had the potential to become one of Chicago's great public spaces."

Visceral. The reporter's first grade teacher told him "gut" was not a polite word, so for the next 12 years, he used "tummy" until he discovered "visceral" in Fiction Writing 101 in college and has used it ever since, as in a visceral feeling or visceral pride.

Visibly moved. Crying or sobbing on the part of a public official or VIP. Regular people are still allowed to cry.

Visitor. The reporter, who is serving a lifetime sentence to never use the term "I" or to identify himself in any other way. The phrase "greeted a visitor" is

a signal to other journalists that the reporter met the interviewee in a really interesting place, such as a remote guerilla hideout, but readers are expected to assume someone other than the reporter has arrived.

Vital Question. A question.

Vivacious . Lively as hell after three Martinis.

Voyeurism. What the print media has to say about televised coverage of sensational news.

Volatile. Explosive. All countries where half the population carries Kalashnikovs.

Vow. Pledge or promise. Usually in headlines, but when used in the story text in political reporting is never followed by, "He refused to put his vow in writing." Reporters may have the vow recorded digitally or on tape, but rarely confront the pol with it a few months later.

{W

firefighters," *The Arizona Republic* reported Apr. 17, 2011.

We are learning more about. "When you hear a TV newscaster start a story with the phrase, 'We are learning more today about...' you may assume a more appropriate phrasing might be, 'In today's *Times-Union* we read that...,'" wrote Rex Smith in the *Albany Times-Union*, April 24, 2011.

Wag. The anonymous wit quoted by the writer. The wag is usually the writer quoting his or her own cynical or supposedly funny lines: "As one City Hall wag observed, 'The city councilor retired because of illness. The voters got sick of him.' "

War chest. A politician's campaign bank account which usually totals at least ten times the amount the office will pay. Reporters rarely mention this fact or ask the candidate, who, of course, demands fiscal responsibility, why he or she will spend millions of dollars to get the lousy-paying job.

Wary. Someone raised a question about something someone else is doing or planning. Countries or people who don't trust the other guys, and with good reason. They view each other with wary eyes.

Was unavailable for comment. Nobody was home when we called. Used when somebody is being accused of misconduct.

Watershed. Important development. Often applied to a political race or legislation but also to an event the reporter figures is significant, even if the word choice is puzzling. "The Rodeo-Chediski Fire will be remembered for years to come as the worst fire disaster to hit the state, but it proved to be a watershed moment for Arizona

Weapons makers. Term used in stories of overcharge and bad performance. If nothing is amiss, they are called "defense contractors."

Weather. Used as a verb, it's to stand up to something strong. Experienced politicians always manage to weather a withering barrage of questions.

Weather beaten. The condition of all seashore cottages. Seashore mansions are never weather beaten, but are majestic or sprawling, or both.

Weigh. What politicians do when figuring out if they can hustle enough contributions to finance a campaign and if voters will have forgotten they were indicted a couple years ago.

Well-groomed. Vain with a touch too-much of after-shave lotion in men, prim and proper in women.

Well-known. So famous the reporter got to tell you. Rod Mickleburgh, of the Toronto *Globe and Mail*, on May 20, 2011, wrote: "The artist, Martin Creed, well-known since winning the esteemed Turner Prize in 2001 for a light flickering off and on in an empty room...." If Creed is "well-known" for that work of art, it would be a real challenge to find words to describe Michelangelo. See also *Famous*.

Well-manicured lawns. Used to describe neighborhoods with high-priced houses and small-minded people. **DEEP TRANSLATION**: Bigotry abounds.

Went awry. Usually an illegal drug deal that went bad.

Went bad. An illegal drug sale that did not end with all parties alive and happy.

Whirlwind. A publicity or fund-raising tour or visit, even though it's slow and dull. "Gov. Deval Patrick is on a whirlwind tour of Washington as part of the National Governor's Association winter meeting, including a White House dinner hosted by President Obama," The Associated Press reported from Boston, Feb. 25, 2012. Also, a week-long celebrity romance that winds up in a quickie marriage in Nevada.

Whisk. "Prisoners and politicians are always whisked from place to place," writes Frank Fellone, of *The Arkansas Democrat-Gazette*. "Never driven. Seldom taken. Often used in conjunction with tarmac, as in whisked from the tarmac."

White stuff. Snow, after the word snow has been used once in a TV weather report.

Wicked. Obligatory in New England media as an adverb or adjective in headlines and features about characters, places, teams, businesses, food, films or whatever wicked local thing is covered.

Widely. Adverb used to strengthen the reporter's opinion, such as widely expected, seen, viewed, considered or believed. Widely is so handy that the authors of *Journalese* have used it more times than they should have in this book.

Widely praised. When referring to a public figure, two people once said he was a good guy who should never have been indicted.

Widely viewed as. The reporter and an editor think the same about it.

Widespread. Anyone's guess, but two or more of something.

Wiggle room. Space to get out of something, such as a politician's vague promise or a reporter's guess. But it is also used when a lack of wiggle room means no money for non-essential family spending.

Willowy. Lithe. **DEEP TRANSLATION**: A model or society lady at least 20 pounds underweight.

Without a scratch. Condition of race car drivers who are not hurt in spectacular crashes.

Withering. Any opposition, ranging from complaints at a town meeting to machine gun fire by the enemy. The Associated Press reported on Jan. 27, 2011, that "withering opposition from hundreds of historians" forced WalMart, which "weathered two years of criticism by preservationists," to drop plans for a Supercenter at the site of the Civil War Battle of the Wilderness in Virginia.

Wonk. Usually used with policy, as in policy wonk. Origin of wonk is debated, but it may have come from wonky, British slang for shaky or feeble, which a lot of wonks' stuff is.

Work cut out for them. What opponents of seemingly unstoppable movements face.

Work together. Editorial writers' favorite admonition meaning you should do what we tell you to do.

Working-class neighborhood. Lawns are not manicured or hedges well-trimmed, but if a tragedy has befallen the area, it is *tight-knit*.

World class. Puffed up term for someone or something. Often used by local media to describe efforts to make the home town a new Paris or London. David Kubiak, a student of Boston's Byzantine politics, would add Kabul to the world class cities that Boston boosters look up to.

World renowned. Even more famous than plain old renowned. The person is so identified because most readers never heard of the guy, as a "world renowned warbler imitator."

Wreak. Obligatory verb to be used with havoc.

Wrecking ball. What demolishes a building even it's done by bulldozers, backhoes, dynamite or careful dismantling. "However, the proposed fast food restaurant is on hold until the Pittsfield Community Development Board decides if Plunkett School should be given a temporary reprieve from the wrecking ball," reported *The Berkshire Eagle*, April 5, 2012.

Wrest. Far more dramatic than grab, take over, snatch, conquer or win. Control is often wrested, whether by one dictator who wrests it from another dictator who was a revolutionary who wrested control from a previous dictator. Or the GOP wanting to wrest control from the Dems, or vice versa. Or a state in the wresting control action, as coloradoan.com reported, Jan 23, 2012, "Lawmakers aim to wrest control of Colorado public lands from Federal government." New York Mayor Michael Bloomberg has been especially busy in efforts to wrest control—of the Brooklyn Bridge Park (*New York Daily News*, Dec 7, 2009), and of city worker pensions (AP story quoted in *Deseret News*, Jan 19, 2001), both

from the state, and "our schools from the hands of the people" (*SocialistWorker.org*, Sept. 1, 2010).

Wrong side of the law. A criminal. Nobody is ever reported as being on the right side of the law.

XYZ}

Yen. Obligatory in a headline or story about Japanese food, restaurants or travel.

Zeitgeist. Reporter shows off his German when meaning the spirit of the time. In praise of the sockeye salmon, seattletimes.com, on Sept. 18, 2010, reported: "It would be hard-pressed to pick a better candidate to capture our have-it-all, eco-wannabe zeitgeist."

Acknowledgments

Thanks for help with this compilation to William Aldridge, Jan Aschan, Russell Ash, Fran Barbieri, Larry Beck, Stu Beck, Cathy Boyd, Paul Clancy (*Washington Star, USA Today, Virginian Pilot*), Susanne Berger, Stanley Bloom, Stephanie Callahan, Walter Carter, Rip Collins, Elizabeth Conner, Matt Conti, Steve Daley, Hal Davis, Diana Dawson, Nigel Duara, James E. Farmer, Vincent F. Filak, Sam Freedenberg, Mike Feinsilber (Associated Press), Justin G. Friedman, Samantha Friedman, Monika Skole Fuchs, Tom Gill, Paul Hagey, Lois Kobb, Patrick Garvin (*Boston Globe* infographics), Joseph C. Goulden (a former reporter for the *Marshall News Messenger, Dallas Morning News,* and *Philadelphia Inquirer*), Fredda Hollander, Kjell Holm, Sarah Protzman Howlett, Arnold R. Isaacs, David Kubiak, Harold Lohr, Sanjoy Mahajan, Bill Mead (former UPI Detroit bureau manager), Erik Mellgren (reporter, *Ny Teknik*, Stockholm), Raymond Nelson, Kristin Netterstrom (Little Rock City Hall Reporter, *Arkansas Democrat-Gazette*), Amy Menefee Payne, John Pekkanen, the late Charles D. Poe, Dan Rapoport, Dorothy Repovich, Marta Sandén, Marty and Roberta Shindler, Courtney Shove, Mark Skole, Naiman Siegel, Jerry Smith, Anthony A. Spleen, David Sprague, Patricia Gallo Stenman, Doug Turner (Washington columnist for *The Buffalo News*), Elaine Viets (*St. Louis Post-Dispatch*), Erin White, Diane White, Paul Wilson, Tony Wynne-Jones, Holly Wyrwich and Matthew Zimmerman. Thanks also to Bill Young for his fine editorial hand which was put into play at various points as this manuscript developed.

Bibliography

Aldridge, James. *The Diplomat*. Little Brown and Co., 1950.

Associated Press. "Journalese Approved by English Professors," Hartford Courant, December 30, 1953. p. 16-D.

Astor, David. "Writing with voice is focus of session (American Association of Sunday and Feature Editors convention)." *Editor & Publisher* 128.44 (1995).

Baker, Russell. "Praising Every Caesar," *The New York Times*, January 16, 1972.

Berry, Mike. "Life Is A Cliché A No-Win Situation, An Uphill Battle That Sounds The Alarm For A Wake-Up Call (If You Know What We Mean), *The Orlando Sentinel*, December 11, 1994.

Collier, Gene. 2010 Trite Trophy: A cliché for all (sporting) seasons. *Pittsburgh Post Gazette*, Dec. 26, 2010.

Copy Kingdom. *American Journalism Review*, 22.4, 2000.

Dickson, Paul. "A Guide to Crisis Journalese," *Playboy*, March, 1987.

Dickson, Paul. "Modern Journalese: An Insider's Guide to What Newsmen Mean to Say." *Washingtonian*, November, 1985, p. 25.

Dudman, Richard. "Journalese is News Writer's Special Lingo." *Bangor Daily News*, Dec 25, 2001.

Evans, Harold. *Editing and Design, Book One: Newsman's English*, Heinemann, London, 1972.

Fellone, Frank. "No Jargon, Please It's Journalese." *Arkansas Democrat-Gazette* March 1, 2011

Greenfield, Meg. "The Real Winners and Loser." *Newsweek*, November 12, 1984. p. 120.

Hart, Jack. "A manner of speaking (avoiding journalese in news reporting) (Writer's workshop) (Column)." *Editor & Publisher*, December 1992.

Hillier, Bevis. "Making the case for Victoriana." A review of *Consuming Passions* by Judith Flanders, *Spectator* Aug. 26, 2006.

Johnson. "Cliché watch: Journalese Blacklist: Hardscrabble." *The Economist*, June 18, 2010.

Karppi, William J. "Nothing Like Journalese." *The Washington Post*. December 27, 1989.

Keleny, Guy. "Errors & Omissions: Uncontrollable outbreak of journalese results in tragedy," *The Independent*, April 10, 2010.

Knight, Robert M. *Journalistic Writing*, Marion Street Press, 2010.

Leo, John. "A Glossary of Reporterspeak." *U.S. News & World Report*, October 3, 1968. p. 63.

Leo, John. "Journalese: A Ground-Breaking Study." *Time*, Sept. 1, 1986. p. 88.

Leo, John. "Journalese for the lay reader." *Time*, Mar. 18, 1985.

Leo, John. *Two Steps Ahead of the Thought Police*, Second Edition, 1998, Transaction Publishers, New Brunswick, NJ, originally published in 1994 by Simon & Schuster.

Leo, John. "Ugly Truths Untold by the Press," *U.S. News & World Report*, September 10, 1990, p. 23.

LaRocque, Paula. "A conversation in 'journalese," Quill Toolbox, Words/Language. *The Quill* 95.7 (2007)

Marsh, David. "Mind Your Language." *The Guardian*, Feb. 14, 2010.

McGovern, Mick. "Is King Rat really a British spy?" *New Statesman*, Sept. 6, 1996.

Moore, Gilbert. "A golden age of bad newspaper writing," http://blogs.redding.com/mbeauchamp/archives/2011/03/a-golden-age-of.html

Mundy, Liza. "Giant Fireball Claims Columnist," *The Washington Post*, October 29, 2000.

Murray, Jim. "Mediaspeak sense and sensibility (fair comment)." *Insight on the News*, Feb. 4, 2002.

Newspeak: "Why the BBC has an 'issue' with problems." *Independent*, London, England, July 3, 2010.

Rachman, Tom. *The Imperfectionists*, Dial Press, New York, 2010.

Rosenblatt, Roger. "Journalism and the Larger Truth." *Time*, July 2, 1984.

Reuters Handbook of Journalism, available online as http://handbook.reuters.com

Sawislak, Arnold. *Dwarf Rapes Nun, Flees in UFO*, St. Martin's Press, New York, 1985.

Siegal, Allan M. and Connolly, William G. *The New York Times Manual of Style and Usage*, Times Books, New York, 1999.

Sowell, Thomas. "They're Twisting Words—Even as We Speak." *Houston Chronicle*, Nov 17, 1985.

Spiegl, Fritz. *Keep Taking the Tabloids: What the Papers Say and How They Say It*. Pan Books Ltd., London, 1983

"The Lounger." *The Critic: A Weekly Review of Literature and the Arts*, London, Nov. 15, 1890.

Whitfield, Graeme. "Calling children 'tots' is a bungle and I'm reacting with fury to slam it now; Home truth." *Western Mail*, Cardiff, Wales, Mar. 1, 2008.

Whitfield, Graeme. Journalese-English Dictionary (first edition), Whitfield's blog on the subject http://blogs.journallive.co.uk/journalblogcentral/2008/02/journaleseenglish-dictionary-f.html#more

Zimmer Ben. "Crash Blossoms." *The New York Times*, Jan. 10, 2010

Zinsser, William. *On Writing Well*. Harper & Row, 1976.